I couldn't put your book down.  y to read and full of wisdom. It will a like to be. Thank you for a great bo

Ri .list

My favorite part of the book is your honesty woven into every chapter. I loved the depiction of your fight with your wife, culminating in the realization that sometimes we just want to be mad and have no desire to be convinced of our lovability. I can relate to that. Your book inspires truth-telling. It is refreshing to hear someone come clean with their feelings. You are a great teacher of love.

Mysti Lee Rudd, Spiritual Teacher

Your book is wonderful. The simplicity in which you address spirituality has helped and comforted me in my quest for myself and God. It is an excellent tool for helping me to learn to love myself and others. You are truly an inspiration and I am grateful for your contribution toward my personal development.

Carol Ann Willmoth - President of CBDI

I think your book is truly great! Congratulations.

Reverend Deborah Olsen

Thanks for your very practical application of inspired truth. Thanks for your sanity.

Walter Starke - Author/Speaker

A friend of mine in California sent me a copy of your book for my birthday and I have enjoyed it very much! I am especially fond of your Questions - and you have some great ones in the book..

Linda Hedquist

I just finished reading your book *Compassionate Living*, and I wanted to tell you that I really enjoyed it! Every chapter was a delicious morsel of wisdom, humor and personal anecdotes. Thanks for putting together a book with such bold honesty; it was wonderful.

Jeannette Darcy - NASA programmer

This book is right on target - - phasers on stun! I'm one of those starship captains who cruises into a relationship on Red Alert, shields up and phasers locked on - looking for the slightest provocation. Boy did I enjoy looking at myself in your book.

Micheal Pierson - Author

Your book is absolutely beautiful. Thank you for your contribution to all of us.

Bruce Garland

Having been a three year student of *A Course in Miracles*, I found your thoughts focused and enlightening. Your presentation of quotes, experiences and self questions is excellent.

JoeAnne Worsham - Bookstore Manager

I so enjoyed your book and I am happy to share it with those I care for. Let me know when your next book is completed. Your message is a blessing.

Debra Ann Culver

This book is wonderful — simple, straightforward and down-to-earth guidance liberally laced with a great sense of humor. I especially like the affirmations that accompany each chapter. This is a book I find myself lending to my friends! It must be time to buy myself a few extra copies!

Judy Anthony

A wonderful, practical guide to peace, love, and prosperity. I find *Compassionate Living* to be a marvelously practical, simple, and yet challenging guide to achieving peace, love, and prosperity in life. I was especially impressed with the practical ideas for applying spiritual principles for our own growth and healing. Equally impressive is Mr. Stefaniak's vulnerability in illustrating his messages with many stories from his own life. This book is a gem waiting to be discovered by serious students of the wonders of life.

Gerald R. Oncken, Ph.D.

Of the many wonderful books written over the last decade to help us have lives that work better, I think this book, *Compassionate Living*, is one of the best! Jerome Stefaniak has a style of writing which is enjoyable and easy to read. Even more importantly, he offers practical suggestions to the reader which he backs up with stories and experiences from his own life, and the lives of people around him. There is an authenticity in his writing and his love of God and the human spirit permeates every page of the book! For anyone who is a student of *A Course in Miracles*, Stefaniak's book is especially engaging. This book is a wonderful gift to yourself and to anyone you care about.

Catherine Gray

I've been reading your book with a friend. It is a joyful book to read and is bringing me many gifts.

Spruce Krause - Massage Therapist/Breath Practitioner

The spiritual and psychological principals in this book have been the cornerstone of our relationship, before and in our marriage. We find that a loving and light-hearted perspective, which the author practices, really helps the "work" we do to nurture and support a life-filled relationship. Combining the ideal with the practical, this book guides you with inspiration and down to earth experience.

Joy and Harry Togesen

This is the most personally revealing, down-to-earth, and absolute funniest journey to self-awareness and love that I have ever read. It is one book I found myself not wanting to put down. It's sure to become a self-help, spiritual *hit*.

Annah Mesko, Book Reviewer for *The Indigo Sun*

Compassionate Living

Everyday
Spirituality

Compassionate Living
Everyday Spirituality

by
Rev. Jerome Stefaniak

Inner Awakenings
Houston, Texas

This book is based on many of the concepts taught in *A Course in Miracles*® and my personal trainings as well as my experience of life and God. The ideas expressed within are **my interpretation** of the concepts of the *Course* and are not endorsed by the copyright holder of *A Course in Miracles*®.

A Course in Miracles® was retypeset in 1992 which included the numbering of all sections, paragraphs and sentences. The quotes I use from the *Course* are identified by the page number from the first edition and then the second edition respectively.

Portions of *A Course in Miracles*® copyright 1975, 1992, reprinted by permission of the Foundation for
A Course in Miracles®

In some cases the names of the people mentioned in anecdotes in this book have been changed. In other cases, I used real names. Which are real and which have been changed will be kept in my heart.

Printed in the United States of America
Cover design by Schmidt Kaye & Co.
Graphic design & layout by Jerry Stefaniak and Ron Kaye

ISBN 0-9638758-3-3

Printed in cooperation with Brockton Publishing Company,
Houston, Texas.
www.brocktonpublishing.com
800-968-7065

For information, write:

Rev. Jerome Stefaniak
11306 Overbrook
Houston, TX 77077

Acknowledgments

Many people helped create this book, in fact, every relationship I had with others did their part in molding me. In particular, I thank Joe and Sandra Heaney who started me on the path of healing; and Phil and Lura Smedstad who continued the growth. They were powerful spiritual teachers in my life. They were people who helped me to become conscious of who I really am and the part I play in my world. They also taught me how to laugh along the way.

I thank the love and support from my parents, who gave me a solid foundation to start my life and the wisdom to continue through the years. I acknowledge what a good example they have been in teaching me that learning never stops and that we are never too old to grow and change. Specifically I thank my father, Joseph, for instilling in me a sense of humor, acceptance and joy. I thank my mother, Jean, for teaching me independence, a love of music, art, and opening to my creativity. Mom, Tom Hanks in *Forrest Gump* said it best. - "You did good, Momma."

And finally, I acknowledge my most personal teacher and friend, my wife, Stav. She has been a wonderful coach, lover, partner and fellow adventurer as we learned together the principles taught in this book.

Thank you all

Introduction

One night, at a Toastmaster's meeting a member was telling us about his passion to write a new book. After writing only a half chapter, though, he realized that he had covered everything he knew in about twenty pages. It made him feel stupid. It made him feel as if he had nothing new to add to the world. He felt — stuck.

That incident got me thinking. I too, have held back my gifts to the world for the very same reasons. I thought,

"I have nothing new to say. Others have said it better. I'm just rehashing old ideas."

Sound familiar? But that night I realized something. I realized that it doesn't matter what we *think* about what we have to say. What matters is saying it! Every one of us is a unique gift to this world. We have our own ways of saying things and we have our own ways of hearing them. I teach classes on *A Course in Miracles* and the biggest lesson that the *Course* repeats, over and over, is to love ourselves no matter what. It teaches that we are already perfect, that the world is a learning tool, and that it is time for us to realize our love, our gifts and the joy that is around. We should not be afraid to share the gifts that we are.

When I teach *A Course in Miracles*, or any other spiritual concept, my main focus is whether people can apply the concepts in their daily lives. As a popular quotation goes, "Use it or lose it." The aim of this book is to provide spiritual ideas and principles for daily use with some personal examples to illustrate how these principles apply.

The book is divided into three sections: *Waking to God*; *On the Path Home*; and *Finding Heaven*. Each section addresses some aspect of learning to accept and appreciate who we are as humans and as citizens of a much larger Universe.

You may read a concept or two that may be upsetting to you. If this happens, just let it go. Don't even try to understand or apply the concept unless you feel there is *some* truth to the statement. If you find yourself really resisting it, notice the resistance, read the statement again and then release it to your higher self. The truth is, many times in my life I have been exposed to ideas that were outrageous, "stupid" and totally dangerous — or so I thought. Weeks, months or years later I found those very same thoughts to be comforting, true and supportive. At the end of each chapter there will be a self discovery quiz or a list of affirmations. These are designed to help you in opening more to your love and in embracing these concepts in your everyday life. In the self discovery quiz, answer each question to the best of your knowledge. There are no right or wrong answers, only awakening. If you are new to using affirmations as a way of changing your thinking, there is a chapter near the end of the book that explains this powerful tool.

Life is not about doing it right every time. It is not about being perfect. I still falter and stumble along the way. But now I know that I no longer have to do it perfect and I no longer have to do it alone. Life is about growing and experiencing and learning — with others. Life is to be enjoyed.

Contents

Waking to God

On the Path Home

Finding Heaven

Waking to God

It is time to wake up to who *we really are*. Most of us have spent years, even lifetimes, being unaware of o ur true nature. We have thought of ourselves as weak, insignificant creatures, never realizing that we are children of a loving God with unlimited creative powers, that our essence is spiritual, and that we are meant to be the masters of our lives. As we become conscious of our part in the world, we receive the means to change our world. But first we have to realize the part we play.

The greatest mistake you can make
is to be continually fearing
that you'll make one.

Elbert Hubbard

You've got to learn
to like yourself first.
I'm a little screwed-up,
but I'm beautiful.

Steve McQueen

You grow up the day you have
your first real laugh —
at yourself.

Ethel Barrymore

Life with Compassion

Years ago, the thought of having compassion for myself and others was alien. I felt that compassion was a "sissy" feeling, a sign of weakness. That was until I read a book by Theodore Isaac Reuben called *Compassion and Self Hate* and I began to see the many ways we hate ourselves and others. I saw the sneaky, suppressed methods we use to keep our lovability to a minimum, to keep us safe from feeling anything uncomfortable. I saw a lot of myself in that book. I have been on a spiritual journey ever since.

What is compassion? Compassion is loving myself right where I am, *no matter what is happening in my life*. Compassion is the ability to see my divinity **and** my humanness in the divine scheme of life. It is the ability to see that the same fears, doubts and demons assail **all** of us and to remember not to judge myself or others for these very aspects. It's the ability that when I am confronted with an aspect of myself that I find repugnant, to remember that I will be uncovering new areas of my life as long as I am on this world, and to take a breath and to love myself anyway. Most important, I believe it's the ability to laugh at ourselves, to see ourselves intertwined in the divine comedy of life.

A Course in Miracles states that all the problems we cause in the world, the fear, the separation, the loneliness from God, happened when the Son of God forgot how to laugh, thinking that somehow he had defied God and now God was *out to get him*. Who is the Son of God? The Son of God is all of us. Not just Jesus Christ but all of our minds and hearts together. Jesus was one part of the Sonship that embodied the spirit of God. He is our elder brother who showed us a new way of looking at life and God.

We are all on a journey back to God, because, truthfully, that is the only place we can go. God created us out of love and only by walking back into love, by having compassion for ourselves, will we find the way. Every step we take, though, is a *human* step, fraught with temptations, mistakes and fears. We must learn to laugh and accept ourselves. We must remember, as Rev. Howard Caesar once told me,

"We are not physical beings trying to have a spiritual experience, but spiritual beings having a physical experience."

Sometimes when people get introduced to the concept that they are totally responsible for their lives, they begin to beat themselves up. They use spiritual principles to judge themselves,

"I must be bad. See! I'm so unspiritual because I am attacking my body with cancer." (Or a cold, or divorce, or whatever.)

Or people believe that praying, doing affirmations or meditating will cure them of disease or keep trouble away. And if those acts don't work, if they get a cold, hurt themselves or create divorce, they then believe that they let themselves down. They believe that they are failures.

This is not compassion. Yes, disease, divorce, strife and troubles are a reflection of our innermost thoughts, but it is still only a reflection. It is an indicator of our suppressed thoughts and beliefs, but it does not change *who we are* one bit! There may be lessons that we are destined to learn and praying may not change the lesson. The lesson we need to learn may be bigger than just our health, relationship status or financial situation. But compassion can change how we *accept* the lesson. I believe that sometimes we create illnesses, not only for ourselves, but also for the people in our lives. I used to wonder why advanced teachers would still create cancer or heart attacks until I realized that none of us knows what gift is being presented in any particular lesson, or even *who* the lesson is for. In my opinion, the challenge is not whether you can love yourself when you have a lot of money, your relationship is perfect and you are healthy. Those are the easy times! The real challenge is whether you can love yourself with cancer, AIDS or even a cold. Can you love yourself for being overweight, smoking, addicted to love? Can you love yourself bagging groceries for a living?

As you are reading this book, stop for a moment and look at your body. Do you like it? Do you enjoy the sensations you can experience with it? Or do you judge its imperfections? Something I realized a few years ago, is that the body I have will be with me until I die. I can't run away from it! I can change some things about it, but mostly, I'm stuck with it, just the way it is. I probably will not grow more hair on my head and I may always struggle with my waistline, but I realized that I did not want to continue hating and judging my body every time I passed a mirror. I realized I had to start appreciating what a wonderful tool it is — not perfect — but still amazingly wonderful.

This doesn't mean that we learn to love our bad habits and just sit there. Life is about change. Life is about growth. The real question is:

"Can you love yourself *along the way* — **as** you change, **as** you grow, **as** you learn?"

Begin to see yourself and others through the eyes of compassion. Compassion is the key that unlocks hearts bound in judgment and prejudice. Compassion is the salve that heals the stinging wounds of the past. Compassion is the sight that allows people blinded by unforgiveness to see with love. Compassion is the warmth that melts the icy fear that keeps us from moving forward in life. Compassion is the coolness that calms the raging anger. Compassion is the great equalizer that shows our connection and similarities to others. Compassion is peace.

Peace is not *out there*, waiting to be discovered and plucked like a ripe fruit. Peace is in our hearts. It is in that holy place that we learn the true value of who we are. It is in our hearts that we reclaim our loving inheritance from God. Check in with your heart and slowly you will see what is the real truth about you.

Self Discovery Quiz

- *When you hear the word "compassion," what is the first thought that occurs to you?*

- *How did your mother express compassion for herself and others?*

- *How did your father express compassion for himself and others?*

- *Do you know of anybody who treats others with compassion? What do you admire or judge about them?*

- *If you treated yourself with more compassion, what are you afraid could happen to you?*

- *Do you have a thought, that if you are not constantly correcting and criticizing yourself, you'll get lax and never grow?*

- *Do you ever acknowledge what you do right to yourself?*

- *When you make a mistake, how long does it take before you forgive yourself?*

- *What is something you secretly love about your body?*

- *When is the last time you treated yourself to something nice, just because you are you?*

Every man has the right to feel —
"because of me was the world created."
The Talmud

The heart of a good man
is the sanctuary of God.
Madame Anne de Stael

To love oneself is the beginning
of a life-long romance.
Oscar Wilde

Some Compassionate Truths About You

- *The body that you have is the one you will experience for life. You can change it or leave it alone. You can choose to love it or hate it. The choice is yours.*

- *You are not alone in this world. There are many people who are willing and able to help you, love you and support you. You can choose to let them love you, or you can shut them out. That is your choice.*

- *There is a loving, caring part of you that yearns to share itself with others. You can suppress it, for fear of being judged, or you can let it out regardless of what others think.*

- *You are a gift to this world.*

- *Until you fulfill your secret desires, you will continue to feel unfulfilled and dissatisfied. Claiming your desires is up to you.*

- *You are wiser than you sometimes realize.*

- *You are given many learning experiences every day. Some are pleasant, some not. Whether you learn from these experiences is up to you.*

- *Any lessons that are not learned will be repeated. These are called "patterns".*

- *You may create many challenges in your life — they can be health challenges, life challenges or even spiritual challenges. Whether you decide to have compassion for yourself is up to you.*

- *You are already whole and complete. You may have forgotten this truth temporarily.*

- *No matter how much you grow, you will still have "good" days and you will still have "bad" days.*

- *As you grow, you will make many mistakes. You can judge and berate yourself, or you can be gentle and love yourself anyway.*

What we are is God's gift to us.
What we become is our gift to God.
Louis Nizer *Brooklyn Law Review*

Who looks outside, dreams;
who looks inside, awakes.
Carl Jung

Argue for your limitations
and sure enough — they're yours.
Richard Bach *Illusions*

With a little doubt,
there is a small awakening.
With great doubt,
there is a great awakening.
With no doubt,
there is no awakening.
Zen saying

The Sleeper Must Waken

We are all asleep — asleep to the magnificence of who we are, asleep to the love all around, asleep to the lessons we can learn daily. In the movie *Dune*, Paul Atreides repeatedly hears his father's voice telling him,

"The sleeper must waken."

A Course in Miracles relates how when we are having a dream or nightmare and then awaken, we accord no reality to the dream. We realize that we were safe in bed all the time, no matter what form of monster or trouble seemed to threaten. Likewise, we are spiritual beings who dream of a world, a world of fear, hate, lack and uncertainty.

God, like any good parent, sees us dreaming, sees that we are troubled and in fear, but to Him, the dream is an illusion. He could wake us, but that would impose upon our free will, which is one of His gifts to us. We are the ones dreaming the nightmare, making up the fear, the hate and the lack. Waking us too suddenly can cause more fear, so He sends His messenger — the Holy Spirit — into our dreams, to gently remind us who we are and to awaken. It is then up to us to decide whether we want to listen.

We've all had wake up calls. They always start as a gentle jingle, a quiet spiritual Post-It note. We notice something that upsets us about our relationship, for example. If we listen and learn, we grow and waken a little more. If not, well, the alarm gets louder and louder until it can virtually blast like a siren.

For example, you notice some unsettling aspects about your relationship (jingle). It's not comfortable addressing these issues (the love may go away!) and so you ignore them. Then other issues appear (the bells get louder), but you continue to ignore them. You tell yourself,

"I don't want to look at this! It may threaten my relationship! I don't want to be alone!"

But the problem doesn't go away, and, until it has been addressed, it grows. After a few months or years of ignoring these messages, denying there is a problem, something breaks. The marriage ends in divorce or the child has to go into drug treatment. Or sadly, the love simply dies, the relationship continues, but just as an empty shell. Now the alarm sounds like a siren.

When we look back on a broken marriage, or a child with drug problems, isn't it true that there were warning signs all along the way? Isn't it true that we could have addressed what was going on earlier? We just weren't brave enough at the time to say what we thought and address the problem. Instead, we hoped it would go away, we hoped the phase would pass, or that the other person would grow up. And day by day, the problem grew until it *demanded* to be handled.

We all do this. The difference, though, between a person who is awake and one who is asleep is that one takes action. The one who is awake goes right into the fear — into the dream (or nightmare), knowing that God is ever present and that even though the situation may look more upsetting and fearful for a while, the final outcome is always love. When we begin to waken, we find that our reality is love. We find that the people in our world are actually loving, caring people, who also want to change, but may also be asleep.

Self Discovery Quiz

- *Is there something about my relationship that **irritates** me, but I don't want to address at this time?*

- *Is there something about my job that **irritates** me, but I don't want to address at this time?*

- *Is there something about my children that **irritates** me, but I don't want to address at this time?*

- *Do I let others persuade me that what I feel is not important?*

- *Do I feel defensive when somebody addresses my weight, my smoking or drinking habits, my job or my relationship?*

- *Do I feel defensive when somebody asks questions about my parents?*

- *Do I feel defensive about my children's performance in school?*

*You cannot escape the responsibility
of tomorrow by evading it today.*

Abraham Lincoln

*Man's mind stretched by a new idea
never goes back
to its original dimensions.*

Oliver Wendell Holmes

*A man can be as truly a saint in a factory
as in a monastery,
and there is as much need of him
in the one
as in the other.*

Robert J. McCracken, D.D.

*"Wonderful sermon!
Everything you said
applies to somebody or other I know."*

Anonymous

No Matter Where You Go, There You Are

A *Course in Miracles* states repeatedly that everything that we perceive (i.e.: see, hear, taste, smell, feel) and every experience that we have originates in our mind. Our minds are powerful tools with which we create the lives we live, the amount in our checking account, the jobs we have and the relationships we keep. Our thoughts and perceptions also determine how we respond to any situation.

If you want to change your life, that change can only occur within your heart. As you change your heart, surprisingly the world *seems* to change also — or the problem simply leaves. But the change must come from within first.

When the Bible says that we are created in the image and likeness of God, it's not being poetic or metaphorical. It is literal. We are children of God and He has endowed us with the same love, power and wisdom. The only difference between ourselves and God is that we did not create God. He created us. Other than that, we are the same. For example, my daughter has just as much potential as I do. She has the same potential to write books, program computers, and create relationships as I do. She also has the potential to create *her* life in *her* way. But basically there is no difference — except that I came first.

What this means is that our minds are constantly creating the world we see. If we believe that the world is cruel, uncaring and vicious, we will notice the cruel, uncaring and vicious aspects of the world. We will expect cruel things to occur, and, being powerful creators, we will draw cruel situations to us. Likewise, if I'm having a good day, and my mind is at peace, I may believe that the world is wonderful, loving and full of caring people. I will notice the loving aspects of my world, attracting wonderful, loving people and experiences. And these situations are as ambivalent as our thinking. One moment the world is fearful, the next loving. Have you ever had a day like that?

 15

When I went to marriage counseling with my second wife, I remember thinking that things would get better once *she* changed. I was convinced that she was the one with the problem so I was resistant to any idea that part of the problem was my creation. Not surprisingly, not much changed in our relationship. Since I wouldn't change my view of her, I ended up leaving her for another woman. And I thought I left my problems behind. I thought they were gone. But there is a saying that I couldn't ignore,

"No matter where you go, there you are."

Well, those problems and situations followed me into the next relationship, and the next and the next. It took me awhile to finally admit that maybe, just maybe, I was part of the problem.

When you look at it objectively, it makes total sense. We have absolutely no control over whether we can affect another person's actions. They may or may not agree with us. They may or may not listen. We can threaten and they may change for a while, out of fear, but ultimately they'll probably revert to the old behavior.

But we do have 100% control over our thoughts and feelings. *A Course in Miracles* says that we are the ones who decide how we respond to any situation. We determine how we want to feel in any situation, and we determine the outcome. Let me give you an example. If you have a thought that men or women cannot be trusted because they always leave, what do you think you will expect to happen when you get into a relationship? The relationship may start wonderful, open and trusting, but after awhile, the old barriers rise up. The fearful thought arises that if this person could see who I *really* am, they would leave. You begin to wonder and worry when this person is going to desert you. You'll look for *signs* that they are thinking of leaving. You may begin checking on what they do, who they have lunch with, etc. Asking questions. Getting angry if they look at another person. Arguments ensue. Your fear grows bigger and so you hold tighter. Your partner begins to feel strangled and what do you think they *probably* want to do? Get away! And, unless the situation changes, unless you look at your own thoughts and feelings of unlovability, your partner will leave.

And to make things even crazier, if, by chance, you do create a relationship with someone who **will not** leave, if you don't address your own issues of abandonment, you'll pick and needle until you convince yourself that there is something wrong with them and then you will leave. Either way, you end up alone. Nobody wins.

I now see that if I am not happy with my life, I am the one who has to change. Not my wife. Not my children. Not the economy. Not the world. But I.

The thought that we are the creators of our world is a very empowering concept to learn. Many of us may resist this thought because we have been taught that we are the victims of the world, victims of outside situations. But once the concept is accepted and grasped, there is no more power that we can ask for. Harnessing the power of our thoughts truly make us masters of our universe. Knowing where the problem lies, then it can be addressed. As the cartoon character Pogo said,

"We have met the enemy, and it is us."

We are the ones causing the upset in our lives. We are the ones choosing to hang onto old hurts and fears and then using them to respond to the circumstances in our lives. Realizing that we are the creator of our life, though, gives us a powerful tool to alter it. From there we begin to claim back our Christhood.

Affirmations

- *Everything I see, hear, taste, smell, feel and think is my idea.*

- *I am now willing to see my world differently.*

- *I now claim responsibility for how I act in all situations.*

- *My world is loving and I am now willing to see that.*

- *As I extend love, so I see it.*

- *As I extend peace, so I see it.*

- *As I extend joy, so I see it.*

- *No matter where I go, there is God.*

- *Wherever God is, so am I.*

- *I am safe.*

"It seems to me," said the judge, *"that you've been coming up before me for the last 20 years."*
"Can I help it," replied the prisoner, *"if you don't get promoted?"*

Anonymous

The soul is dyed with the color of its thoughts.

Marcus Aurelius

When we have shut all the world out, we find that we have shut ourselves in.

William Graham Sumner

When a man blames others for his failures, it's a good idea to credit others with his successes.

Howard W. Newton

The Blame Game

When I say that we create everything in our lives, what I mean is that we *invite* people in our lives to act out whatever lesson we need to learn. It doesn't mean that we **make** people be alcoholics or act abusive, but that we invite them into our experience to teach us. Maybe we invite abuse so that we can learn to be assertive and to set our boundaries. Maybe we invite alcoholism so that we can look at our own co-dependancies and addictions. Maybe we invite unfaithfulness so that we can look at our own issues of trust. Everybody has their own agenda to learn and everybodys' lessons are different, but most of the time, we don't want to admit to the lessons we most need to learn.

So we use blame in an effort to not look at what we think is inside of us. This is what *A Course in Miracles* calls **projection**. Projection is the concept that, if I see something inside of me that I don't like, and, if I can throw it onto somebody else, then I think that I have gotten rid of it. This is one of the ego's tools to not take responsibility. As long as it can blame everybody else for its problems, nothing has to change.

But projection never works! Because when you throw off those judgments of yourself onto the world, what do you think you *see* in the world? Those same judgments you thought you escaped, staring right back at you! Only now they are in the form of other people or actions or jobs or even countries. It is like living in a beautiful mansion, but using the front yard for your garbage dump. Whenever you look out, all you see is garbage, and the world does look pretty bleak from that standpoint.

The opposite of projection is extension. Extension allows. Extension accepts. What we do when we extend is that we look inside our True selves, and see that we **are** love, we **are** joy and we **are** peace. It may take some time to learn this, but that is our purpose here anyway. And from that basis, we extend the same thoughts and feelings to the world. We invite others into our experience instead of keeping them out.

Of course, when we do this, what we see in the world is joy, love and peace. And it is catching. As you begin to see the world differently, you respond differently and as you respond to the world differently, the world responds to *you* differently. It goes around and around. If you see and expect peace and forgiveness in others, that is what you will see and receive in return. If you expect attack and hatred, that too will be your reward. Just as the ego has used projection effectively to promote discord and pain, so we can use extension as a way to promote peace and joy.

How do you know if you are projecting? Whenever you get upset about anything in your world, know that at some level you are trying to throw off some unresolved, unlovable aspect of yourself onto the world. When we see people *out there* doing things that touch unfelt feelings of hurt, anger, shame or guilt, they activate old feelings. If we are unwilling to look at those feelings, we will try to get rid of them. We will project. We will blame.

Sometimes when people are introduced to the idea that they are the creators of their problems, they begin to blame themselves.

"I'm so stupid! I should have known better. Why did it take me fifty years to realize this?"

Blaming ourselves **does not work**. It is no different than blaming the world, except now it's turned inward. Now we are attacking ourselves instead of the world. This is where we need to exercise compassion. The only way to develop compassion for yourself is to practice it, especially when you think you don't deserve it. So right now, before you proceed I want you to stop and take a slow, deep breath. Let your mind relax from all the yammer, yammer and tell yourself,

"I now accept myself just the way I am."

"I am not yet perfect and God does not expect me to be perfect."

"I now love myself just the way I am, knowing that I am also changing into a more loving, compassionate person."

And ask yourself this question. When Jesus was training for His ministry on Earth, did He experience fear at times? Did He ever have doubts? Did He cry? Did He feel anger at times? Did He ever judge Himself, even briefly? Did He forgive Himself for His lessons?

I think so. I think the greatest lesson we can learn from Jesus is that He too was a man, with all of the human doubts, fears and failings. But He overcame them, to be an example for all of us that it is possible.

Remember,

"No matter where you go, there you are."

You can choose to love yourself or judge yourself at any moment. The choice is yours.

Affirmations

- *I now love myself for the loving, divine person I really am.*

- *I now accept my lessons with grace, love and compassion for all.*

- *I no longer blame myself for blaming others.*

- *There is no reason good enough for me to hate myself any more..*

- *I learn from every mistake because I am teachable.*

- *I now choose life!!!*

- *I now bless the God in me and I bless the God in others.*

- *It is safe for me to accept myself.*

- *The more I love and accept myself, the more the world accepts me.*

Children are natural mimics —
they act like their parents
in spite of every attempt to teach
them good manners.

Anonymous

Every child comes with the message
that God is not discouraged of man.

Rabindranath Tagore

All children are born good.

Lord Palmerston

I do look up and communicate lovingly
with my friend up there. . .
although I know God is within.
I look up and laugh and live.

Mary Martin

Remembering Our God Within

L et me tell you a true story about all of us. When we were born, this is how we looked:

Conscious

We were physical representations of God (we still are, we just forgot). Have you ever looked into a baby's eyes? There is no suspicion or expectation there. There is just love and acceptance. A baby actually expects only the best from the world. They are fully conscious and totally in the present. When they are hungry, they cry, when they are angry, they scream, when they are happy, they coo and gurgle and when they are sleepy, they sleep. A baby has no judgments, about itself or the world. When it has to go to the bathroom — it poops. No thought, no judgment — just action. Totally in the present. I have never seen a baby who worried about the mortgage, how to pay for college or where the car payment will come from.

Now comes the sad part. As children we made only one mistake. Because we were little and because our parents (and everybody else) were bigger than us, we thought that they must be gods. We thought they knew everything. And being the trusting souls that we were, we believed everything we heard — literally. When our parents said something in anger, we believed that it was true and that it was **our** fault. We may have heard things like:

"See what you made me do?"

"I wish you were never born."

"Why can't you be like your sister? She's always good."

"It would be so much easier if we didn't have an extra mouth to feed."

"You're always underfoot!"

"I didn't say that, dear. You must have imagined it. But let's not tell mommy anyway, OK?"

"Shut up! Dammit! Must you always make so much noise!"

And we are torn. Torn between what we think we saw or heard and what the world is telling us we saw or heard. Torn between what we inherently *know* is right or wrong, loving or cruel and what others tell us. Torn between life, joy and trust versus fear, judgments and hate. We begin to assume that **we** must be mistaken. We assume we must be the broken, malfunctioning part. And being egocentric, we think that everything that happens in our family relates to us. If our parents divorce, we think it's our fault. If mommy is sad, we think that only if we can do better in school, she will get better. We think that if only we weren't so bad, daddy wouldn't be so angry all the time and hurt mommy.

Nobody told us that sometimes our parents were just upset in the moment, and lashed out in anger, never realizing that we believed them totally. Nobody told us that our parents were human and made mistakes just like everybody else. And so, after awhile, the pain of looking at the things we heard (*"I'm in the way, I'm a burden, I'm too loud, I cause trouble"*) became intolerable and we did what any normal child does. We began to suppress those painful thoughts and feelings. We no longer wanted to be conscious all the time and so we pushed those painful thoughts and feelings down. We actually split into two minds — a conscious and an unconscious mind. We looked like this:

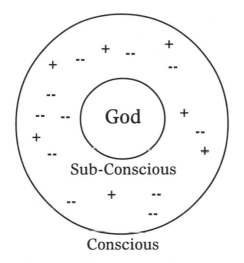

This is the point that psychologists call "the split". This is also the place that *A Course in Miracles* calls "the separation". It is the place where we stop being who we really are, and begin acting the way we *think* others want us to act. It is a separation from our Godhood. This is actually a reenactment of the story of the Garden of Eden — the separation from God. We are still God, but now there is a layer of subconscious thoughts and feelings obscuring our view and we think we have lost our Godliness. The suppressed thoughts and feelings are both positive and negative. And then there is the conscious layer — a thin outer area that we work with every day. These are the thoughts that we are conscious of, but they represent only a tiny portion of our total consciousness. Since we create with our thoughts, it's important to remember that **all** of our thoughts create. Not just the conscious ones. Because we are created in God's image, we create what we see *out there* to conform with what we believe *in here*. No matter what we believe, whether it makes sense or not, we create!

Have you ever had the experience of wanting something and not getting it? Let's say you want a wonderful, loving, passionate relationship. Everything you try just doesn't work. No matter how nice you try to **act**, somehow you end up wrecking the relationship. Why? Remember —

all of our thoughts create. Not just the conscious ones. It has been estimated that the normal person has between 40,000 to 50,000 thoughts per day and most of them are negative, critical, self talk. So trying to change our outward behavior, while it may work temporarily, ultimately gets negated by the unconscious thoughts that we *really* believe. It's like building a house on sand. The foundation keeps washing away.

Let me give a personal example. When I was growing up, I received many spankings. My mom and I seemed to always be at odds over whether I would do what was right or what I wanted to do. Most of the time I did what I wanted to do, thereby leading to the inevitable conflict. Whenever I was about to be spanked, my mother would ask,

"Do you know why I'm doing this?"

"No, why?"

"Because I love you."

Now, I **know** that my mother loved and cared for me and she was afraid that I would become a juvenile delinquent. But as a child, I believed *everything I heard*. Literally. Later in life, I found myself in relationships with women — women who tended to hurt me, have affairs, judge me. I attracted a lot of angry women. In fact, I was subconsciously attracted to angry women. And so I wandered from relationship to relationship, always wondering why women were such bitches. You see, I had this suppressed thought from childhood, that *"if you love me, you will hurt me"* and so I searched for a woman who would love me the way I expected to be loved. That's not the message my mom was saying but it is the one I learned.

I was subconsciously attracted to women who would hurt me because I thought that was what love looked like. I had love and pain wired together. But when I was in a relationship with a woman who hurt me, I didn't like being hurt — nobody does, and so I judged her, got even and left. The real crazy thing, though, is when I created relationships with women who did not hurt me, women who were loving and accepting — well — that didn't *feel* like love and so I judged them, I hurt them, and I left. With all those suppressed thoughts and feelings, there was no way that women could ever win with me.

Another reason I was attracted to angry women was that I had a lot of unresolved anger myself. I had no idea how to express my anger. I was totally afraid of it. But my Divinity (my true self) wanted to be whole. It demanded that I address it. It was as if I had a psychic sign on my back saying,

"I'm angry. Help me. Piss me off, please"

And so I attracted lots of obliging women who played their part, while I thought it was **them** all along. Ultimately the pain of continually breaking up took its toll and I reached a point where the pain got too bad, where I couldn't stand the thought of suffering through another relationship like that. I was tired of being hurt and hurting others. I was tired of being blamed and blaming others. I was tired of always waiting for something bad to happen. I was tired of not being able to trust women. I felt that **anything** was better than this. I was ready to change. Now the Holy Spirit had an open ear to whisper into.

What did I do? I got help. I got into breath integration, a form of therapy that allows suppressed thoughts and feelings to come into our consciousness so that they can be released. I learned how I had love and pain wired together and I learned how to separate them. I learned how to have new relationships with women. I learned that it was OK to "hate" my mom, to be angry, to scream, to cry, to let out all those forgotten hurts, so that the people in my life no longer had to pay for somebody else's past deeds. I had to **learn** what love looked like, how it felt. And I began to create women in my life who taught me lovingly and gently that it was safe to open up to love. That I wasn't going to get hurt. That love **and** life are safe.

Who are we? We are co-creators alongside God. We have the capability to create heaven on this earth. Or hell. But the truth about us has never changed. We may try to convince ourselves that we are sinners, that we are guilty for past misdeeds, that we are unworthy of love, but the truth is, we are always God. He sees us dreaming these nightmares and He sees us in pain and wants to help, but it's **our** illusion. We are ones that need to change.

It's time to wake up to our magnificence. It's time to remember our Father within. And in remembering Him, we regain our life and our joy.

Self Discovery Quiz

- *What were you taught as a child who God was or where God exists?*

- *What would your life look like if you reminded yourself everyday that you are God in a body?*

- *How would God treat your relationship?*

- *How would God act at your job?*

- *In what ways can you express your godliness in your job?*

- *In what ways can you express your godliness with your relationship?*

- *In what ways can you express your godliness even at the grocery store?*

- *Do you know of a person that displays "God in action?" What is it that they do that makes you feel this?*

- *If you surrendered to God within, what do you fear would be asked of you?*

- *Would God ask anything of you that would hurt you?*

*As William Dean Howells and Mark Twain
were coming out of church one morning,
it began to rain heavily.
"Do you think it will stop?" ask Howells.
"It always has," answered Twain.*

*Although the dark of night can conceal the
world, it also reveals a whole universe.*
Anonymous

*When fate knocks you flat on your back,
remember she leaves you looking up.*
Anonymous

*If all of our misfortunes were laid in one
common heap, whence everyone must take
an equal portion, most people would be
content to take their own and depart.*
Socrates

Breakdown or Breakthrough

Have you ever done affirmations, read self-help books, or taken workshops to improve yourself and after a while felt *worse* than when you started? Have you ever done self esteem affirmations to boost your morale and self esteem but after a week really felt like scum? Have you ever taken a prosperity workshop and that week you got unexpected bills, the car broke down and the IRS wanted an audit? It's at times like this when we are tempted to break down and quit.

"This stuff doesn't work. I give up. I'm going back to the way of thinking that's comfortable for me."

Take heart! You're on the verge of a breakthrough! It is usually at this point that people pull back their power, stop the affirmations, stop praying — right at the time when they need to just push through that final yard.

Remember the little God picture from the last section? The one with the subconscious? Well, when we do anything that supports our Divinity, such as affirmations, personal growth, therapy, praying, etc., the God in us begins to grow. It begins to expand. And as it expands, it pushes into our awareness our subconscious thoughts.

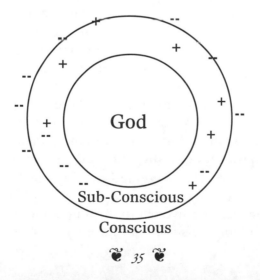

We begin to become conscious of thoughts and feeling that have been hidden for years — some positive, many negative. It may not feel comfortable, but it's actually a time to celebrate. Because now we see how we **really** feel about ourselves, how we **really** feel about relationships, how we **really** feel about money. Once we are aware of our subconscious thoughts, we then have a grasp on what we have to change.

This is the moment of **breakdown** or **breakthrough.** At this point we are sorely tempted to break down and say that these new thoughts are causing the trouble, that loving and believing in yourself does not work. Just remember, though, it's the **old** thoughts that are being activated and acted out. Those thoughts are like the ripples that fan out from a tossed stone in a quiet pond, we need to outlast the ripples, the delayed effects of past beliefs.

Florence Skovill Shinn in her book *The Game of Life and How to Play It* mentions that spirit is **never** late, though many times it may seem to come at the eleventh hour, at the last minute. Time does not exist to our spiritual selves. So we need to persevere through the times when it feels as though nothing we do is working.

Six years ago, I was going through a very accelerated course in personal growth. I was in the process of becoming a Breath Integration Practitioner and counselor. In order to graduate, it was necessary that all of us practitioners look intimately at every part of our selves, at any part that hid pain, shame, anger and hurt. We were continually exposed to the thoughts and feelings that most of us prefer to keep hidden. I went through a long period of self hatred, low self esteem and feeling like an outcast from society. I didn't like what I saw inside and no matter what I did, I still felt horrible and depressed. Luckily I had teachers and friends who supported me through this period. They kept reminding me that this feeling was temporary and I just needed to wait it out until I got to the other side.

During this period, I created moving out from my relationship and having no place to live. Friends took me in and for a period of ten weeks, I lived at different people's houses. I felt rootless, like a bum. I also did not have a job or money, and my counseling career was stuck. I had nothing. Coming home one night after class, my car's brakes squealed with an ominous "metal on metal" sound every time I touched them, and there was radiator fluid leaking into the passenger side of the car. I cried all the way home.

"This stuff sucks! This stuff doesn't work. There is no God. God's abandoned me!"

I arrived at my friend's home, depressed, scared and angry. Later, I was still feeling sorry for myself as I cooked some pork and beans for my supper, when John, my friend, walked in. I don't remember exactly what it was I said but it was some kind of sad, "woe is me" joke. He laughed,

"You know," he said, "it's great to see that you can still laugh, after all that's been going on."

Unexpectedly, something inside me shifted slightly. I looked up and smiled,

"Well, if I can't laugh at myself now, if I can't love myself now, I'll never be able to."

And then that something inside me snapped and I suddenly got it. There was no reason good enough to judge myself anymore. There was no reason good enough to hate myself. It was **my choice** to feel rotten! I could decide how I wanted to feel! I could decide to worry about the car and the money or I could love myself anyway! In that moment my life changed. I had a breakthrough. I decided that no matter what, I was going to love myself, the best way I knew how. When I didn't have money, I loved myself by taking bubble baths, reading in the park, or hanging out with friends. I got a part time job to see me through the beginnings of my counseling career. I got a small loan from my dad to fix the car and find a place to live. And as I received more and more money, I remembered to give some to myself, to constantly remind myself that I was loving, deserving and safe. In the community, I became the person people would call whenever they felt down and stuck because they knew that I would come up with some way to appreciate themselves.

That was a breakthrough. I remember how close I was to a breakdown and how close I was to a breakthrough. It could have gone either way.

Now, when I go through periods of doubt or low self esteem, I have a little mantra that I repeat over and over,

"This too, shall pass; this too, shall pass."

Which are you going to have, a breakdown or a breakthrough?

You decide.

Affirmations

- *There is no reason good enough to judge myself anymore.*

- *I now surrender to my lessons.*

- *When life looks low, I'm getting ready to grow.*

- *I am a winner and I push through to the end.*

- *I reap the benefits of my lessons.*

- *Since I am of God, I am always safe.*

- *I love my lessons, because I learn from every one.*

- *Life is easy as I take my steps.*

- *As I get squeezier, Life gets easier.*

The dark or sick days need not be seen
as bad days,
for they often prompt
our deepest reflection and,
in some cases,
a change of life-style.
In this sense, then,
one can look upon darkness or disease
not as an end but as a beginning of growth.
Eileen Rockefeller Growald

Poverty is uncomfortable;
but nine times out of ten
the best thing that can happen
to a young man is to be tossed overboard
and compelled to sink or swim.
James A. Garfield

If people would dare to speak to one
another unreservedly there would be a good
deal less sorrow in the world a hundred
years hence.
Samuel Butler, *The Way of All Flesh*

Thank You, Sergeant Foley!

When we are not in touch with our divine nature, when we think we have to do it all by ourselves, there is a part of us that feels denied. Because deep down, we know what we really want and how we really want to be. We're just afraid to claim it. But suppressing our aliveness and joy causes us pain, and so, in an effort to break the deadlock of fear versus love, sometimes we create hard lessons.

In the movie *An Officer and a Gentleman,* Zach Mayo meets up with Sergeant Foley in flight officer's training school for the Navy. It is Foley's job to make sure that every officer candidate is capable, train-able, loyal and a credit to his/her country. As he says to the incoming candidates in the first ten minutes of the movie,

"I will use any means, both fair or unfair, to trip you up, to see if you are lacking in any capacity as a future naval a-vi-a-tor."

And he makes their lives hell. He taunts, he pushes, insults and challenges every part of their lives. Now, Zach is a slick cookie. He's had a lot of hard knocks in life and so he runs everything *his* way. An absent, distant father and a dead mother taught him to never trust anyone, because, sooner or later, they'll hurt you. He's always looking for the short cut, the easy way. He's a loner, a hustler. He lets nobody in and nobody trusts him. At the flight school, he secretly has an enlisted man shine extra brass buckles so that he can sell them to the other candidates before any inspection. But Foley is no fool.

Just before a weekend leave, Foley discovers Zach's private stash and demands his D.O.R. — to be "dropped on request" — to quit. Zach refuses.

"Put on your fatigues, Mayo. After this weekend, you'll give me your D.O.R."

And Foley puts Mayo through constant hell. Push ups in the mud, endless exercises while being sprayed with water, and constant badgering. Remarks about his father being a "whore chaser and an alcoholic" and his mother committing suicide are rubbed in Mayo's face.

The following day, Zach is doing eternal sit ups as Foley once again attempts to break him.

"Look, Mayo, you'll never be officer material. Why don't we just end this little charade, give me your D.O.R. and we'll go have a beer at TJ's?"

"No sir! I'm not gonna quit!"

"Why would a slick, little hustler like you want to put yourself through all this abuse?"

"I wanna fly jets, sir!"

"My grandma wants to fly jets! I'm talking about character, Mayo."

"I've changed, sir. This candidate believes he would be a good officer, sir!"

"Sell it to the Air Force, Mayo! Give me your D.O.R."

"No sir!"

Foley stands up, tapping his cane on the pavement.

"Give me your D.O.R. Spell it for me, Mayo, D. — O. — R. Dropped on request!"

"No sir! I won't give up. No SIR!"

"Come on, Mayo — D.O.R.!"

"I'm not gonna quit, sir!"

"Alright then! You're finished! You're OUT!"

And Foley spins on his heel and starts to walk away.

"Don't you do it!!" screams Zach. "DON'T YOU DO IT!"

"What did you say?" asks Foley.

And Zach's barriers begin to crack. He sobs and barely looking at Foley says,

"I got no where else to go. . . I got . . . nowhere . . . else . . . to go."

He lowers his head and sobs, "I got nothin'."

Zach has finally met someone in his life who was willing to break through the facade of the tough, little hustler into the part that is hurting and scared. The part that wants to fly more than anything in the world. And Zach finally realizes how important his dream is and he doesn't want to waste this chance. Zach's barriers have been breached and now Foley can teach him. Foley sees this.

"Get up, Mayo. You got some latrines to clean."

Nothing more is said but from then on, Zach begins to see the other candidates as a team and he begins to care. He begins to realize that his life is intertwined with theirs, that he needs to open up and trust others, even if it does hurt.

What happened to Zach in boot camp is exactly what happens to all of us in life. In fact, the divine aspect of our being will search for a Sergeant Foley because we secretly **demand** it! We are all Zach Mayo's. We all have an area where we are slick, we dodge the rules, play our own game, have our own agenda. We think we know better than God. We know what we want and we will manipulate and control our way into getting it.

But all that manipulation only creates fear and pain. Fear at being discovered and the pain of living our lives divorced from our true energy and life. We spend more time "rigging" the game than actually playing it! And that is tiring. As time goes by, the little games and manipulations work less and less. People catch on sooner to our control. We get more fearful until finally we create a Sergeant Foley in our lives — maybe in the form of divorce, being thrown in jail for a D.W.I., discovering our lover having an affair, cancer, whatever. Hopefully, we break. Hopefully, we reach that point where the pain is too terrible and anything is better than this. My second divorce was my Sergeant Foley. After years of controlling others, after years of *acting* loving but never *being* loving, after years of playing my game, I could no longer go on. The pain of hurting others and myself was too great. At that point I remember telling myself,

"There's got to be a better way."

And at that moment, the Holy Spirit had an open door. At that moment I was willing to see that *maybe I* was the one with the problem. Not everybody else. Though it was hard at the time, the cost of letting go of my games and control was a better life and loving relationships.

At the end of the movie, Zach tells Foley,

"I wouldn't have made it without you. I'll never forget you."

Who were the Sergeant Foley's in your life? What people or incidents challenged you, stretched you, pulled you to the breaking point, and when you thought you couldn't stretch anymore — stretched you even further? What did you learn from the experience?

When you receive the gift that was presented, no matter how it looks at the time, at that moment, you too will be able to say,

"Thank you, Sergeant Foley."

Affirmations

- *I may be in fear but I am not in danger.*

- *I now receive the gifts from all my lessons.*

- *I am no longer afraid to confront myself.*

- *The more I see who I am, the more lovable I become.*

- *I no longer see any value in being separate from others.*

- *People can be trusted because I can be trusted.*

- *I have been loved in many ways and many forms.*

- *Just because some people do not love me in the way I think is correct, it does not mean that they do not love me.*

Do I believe in resurrection?
Of course I do!
Every day I see people bringing back to life
old, dead issues.

Jerry Stefaniak

It is not hard to find the truth;
what is hard is not to run away from it
once you have found it.

Etienne Gilson

Every man should keep a fair-sized
cemetery in which to bury
the faults of his friends.

Henry Ward Beecher

The present time has one advantage
over every other. It is our own.

C. C. Colton

Ghosts from the Past

Have you ever met somebody and instantly liked them? For no reason at all? Or, conversely, have you ever met somebody for the first time and instantly disliked them? You can't put your finger on it, but there is *something* that you just hate about them.

That is an example of being affected by a ghost from your past. For example, we meet a new woman and let's say she subconsciously reminds us of Aunt Martha, who was gentle, loving and always kind to us. Instantly we like this new person. We don't know why, we just do. What is happening is that we are reacting to that person as if the original person were present.

Or we meet our new boss, who subconsciously reminds us of Uncle Ralph, who made fun of us, hit us and degraded us. We instantly dislike our new boss, for reasons that we aren't aware. In either case, we are not relating to the person who is there — we are relating to somebody from our past and we will react to this new person *as if* they were that ghost from long ago. We will not be talking to our boss, we'll be talking to Uncle Ralph. At some forgotten level we expect our boss to degrade us, hurt us and somehow, make fun of us. We will always be on our guard. Unfortunately, our boss may just be a wonderful guy and all the while he's wondering why we're so uptight around him. Of course, we may remind him of somebody from *his* past and so he'll relate to us as if we were that person from long ago.

What we have, ultimately is two people, relating to each other through people who are long gone and wondering all the while what's wrong with the other person.

It's a miracle that people can relate at all! With all those ghosts floating around, I'm amazed that many relationships survive as long as they do. So how can we exorcise these ghosts from our world? The first step is to become aware that this is happening.

When you find yourself becoming excessively angry over a situation, madder than the occasion warrants, know at that point that there is more going on than just the story in front of you. As *A Course in Miracles* says,

> *I am never upset for the reason I think.*

Workbook Lesson 51

When I was growing up, my mom and I were always at odds with each other. She was busy trying to raise a child, I was busy trying to do what I wanted to do. In desperation, she called me names and lectured and spanked me. Her favorite word was "fool." I grew up *hating* that word. Every time I heard it, I would feel my spine crawl and my insides tighten with hurt and rage.

One day, years later, my first wife, Marge, and I were at a park, having a mild disagreement about some innocuous issue. At one point, though, she said that I was "just being foolish." I flew into a rage and pretty soon, what started out as a small disagreement turned into World War III. I said things in anger and attack. I wanted to hurt her bad.

It wasn't until days later that I realized who I was really angry at, who I really wanted to hurt — my mom. It was still more years to come before I was willing and ready to address those old issues with my mom. Until then, I was hostage to those ghosts from the past and would suffer in my relationships with women.

We are never upset for the reason we think. We see the world through our eyes, through our past experiences, through our filters. And then we color what we see with the hues and shade of past hurts. When you find this happening to you, as soon as you remember, ask God to help you to "see this situation through Your eyes, not mine." Then be *willing* to see this person differently. Be willing to ask yourself,

"Through what old glasses am I seeing this?"

And then release it to God's Holy Spirit. Note: You don't even have to **want** to see the situation differently. All it takes is the *willingness* to see it differently.

Just be willing — and let God do the rest of the work.

Self Discovery Quiz

- *Do you find yourself sometimes "flying off the handle" over trivial occurrences? What is really going on?*

- *Who in your life today reminds you of your father?*

- *Who in your life today reminds you of your mother?*

- *Who in your life today reminds you of a brother or sister?*

- *Whose voice do you hear when your relationship disapproves of you?*

- *Whose voice do you hear when your boss disapproves of you?*

- *Whose voice do you hear when your relationship **approves** of you?*

- *Whose voice do you hear when your boss **approves** of you?*

*Insanity is doing the same thing
over and over,
but expecting different results.*

Alcoholics Anonymous

Habits are at first cobwebs — then cables.

Anonymous

*Those who do not study history
are doomed to repeat it.*

Anonymous

*I got a book on obsessive-compulsive
disorders. It's great!
I've already read it 623 times.*

Anonymous

Character is simply a habit continued.

Plutarch

Patterns — Nature's Way of Saying *"You're in a Rut"*

S omebody once said,

"A rut is merely a grave with both ends kicked out."

Ever notice those times when you end a relationship and you realize that this relationship was just like the one before? Do you find yourself constantly involved with the same type of person (alcoholic, abusive, angry) no matter how hard you try?

I think it was Carl Jung who once said,

"After the age of thirty, all problems are spiritual."

I believe what he meant was that after we have had enough time to "bump" into life, create our mistakes and lessons, there comes a time (hopefully) that we begin to realize that there is a bigger reason going on behind the scenes. We keep creating the same problem over and over because *we want it.* Now, I want you to know that we are **not** crazy. But there is a reason for this. There is something that we want to learn, something we want to understand and only this lesson will accomplish it.

When you find yourself in a rut, ask yourself,

"Why am I creating this situation?"

*"Why do I **want** this person in my life?"*

"What is the lesson I am trying to learn?"

When we ask ourselves questions like this, our powerful minds begin to work on formulating an answer. But don't be surprised if at first there seems to be no answer. **Our ego does not want us to look within.** It does not want us to question ourselves. It is happy keeping us on the merry-go-round of life — looking for love in all the wrong places — searching but never finding. But remember, **all** of our thoughts create the world we see — not some, but all of them. By asking ourselves these questions, we begin to acknowledge the subconscious areas of our minds. When we look within, when we tell ourselves the truth, that we are still powerful, wonderful children of God, and that there is a reason that we desire this situation, answers will come, at first as a trickle and then as a flood.

In my example earlier of my relationships with women, I created the same pattern over and over — angry women everywhere I went. When I finally took responsibility and asked why I *wanted* these women in my life, I began to get answers such as:

"You don't deserve a loving woman. You were so hard on mom."

"You *are* guilty. You need to be punished."

"Just who do you think you are?"

"Well you're pretty pissed yourself, Jerry. You need to feel this and let it go."

Getting into a relationship with me was a crazy experience for the woman involved. I would be open, loving and vulnerable — at first — but once I was **in** a relationship, once I started to love and care for her, I changed. I would become fearful. I would be afraid that she would see the unlovable parts of me and leave. And so I would suddenly change from an open, vulnerable type of guy to a warrior, bracing for battle. I would approach this new era of my relationship somewhat like Captain Kirk of Star Trek approaching a Klingon battle cruiser.

"Mr. Sulu. Put us on red alert, shields on full and have the crew set their phasers on . . . kill. And Scotty, have impulse power ready so we can leave on the first impulse. Now. . . let's relate."

And all the while, Scotty was screaming in my mind,

"We can't take much more of this Captain. We're gonna break up. I'm sure of it!"

Over and over I would create the same scenario. And over and over I acted the same way. Sound familiar?

So how do we break out of patterns? Most of us assume that if we do just the opposite, we'll break the pattern. I once was talking to a woman who informed me that she had no relationship issues. She had finally handled them.

"That's great!" I said. "What did you do?"

"I stopped getting into relationships."

That is **not** an example of handling a pattern. What she is doing is simply avoiding whatever lesson is just begging to be taught. To handle a pattern requires a conscious decision to look at your part of the pattern. How are you attracting these people into your life? What is your payoff?

I found myself attracted to angry women, partly because I was angry and partly because I thought that love looked like pain. When I tried to negate the pattern by being with women who weren't angry, do you know what I discovered? I wasn't attracted to them! They didn't light my fire like an angry, passionate woman did. At that point I felt stuck. I could be in a relationship that was boring (slow death) or I could be in a relationship with an angry, attacking bitch (quick death). Either way, we would both lose.

How did I break the pattern? First by telling myself the truth.

"Jerry, you *like* being with angry women!"

"But I don't like being hurt and attacked," I responded in defense.

"That's true, but what is it about angry women that turns you on?"

"Well, it's not the anger per se. It's the passion. It's the fire. They're alive. They're fun."

What I began to see was that there were aspects that angry women possessed that I wanted to possess. Like telling the truth. Like asking for what they wanted. Like living life with passion and *"Damn the torpedoes — full speed ahead!"* What I didn't like were the negative, attacking aspects of anger. And these were the very issues I had to deal with.

You see, I was afraid of my anger because deep down inside I felt that if I let all that rage out, I would become like my mother — the mother I still saw in my mind and never forgave — the angry, hurtful mother. But by not releasing the anger and hurt I felt around growing up, I perpetuated it in my life, day by day. So I allowed myself to begin to feel my hurt toward my mom, my anger, my rage. Not by myself, mind you, but with support of counselors and friends.

I learned to no longer be afraid of my anger but to use it to propel me into action. Propel me into telling my truth. Propel me into my passion for life. And as I lit my fire of passion for life, I found that I could be with passionate, fiery women and we both could have fun. But I had to light **my** fire first. And once I lit my own fire inside, I stopped getting burned.

Another payoff for this process was that my relationship with my mother changed. I began to see and understand the fear she had, trying to raise us kids correctly. I began to understand her frustration of not doing the things **she** wanted to do — always putting the family first and feeling unacknowledged. It didn't diminish the anger that I had to feel, but I began to see her less as MOM and more as a person. A person who had feelings, and love, and dreams, and wishes — like everybody else. A person who had fears, and doubts, and worries — like everybody else. Over time we have been able to talk about those hard years, the guilt, the frustration, the pain, and I have truly come to love my mother more than I ever thought possible.

Not surprisingly, my relationships with women improved. Now, this is the kind of pattern I can live with!

Affirmations

- *I no longer judge myself for the patterns I create. I learn from my mistakes, day by day.*

- *I am now willing to create patterns that bring me joy and prosperity.*

- *Changing and learning are easy for me.*

- *I release old patterns with ease and love.*

- *I am now aware of lessons coming my way and I learn more quickly, without struggle.*

- *I become more aware of my patterns because I am not afraid to see.*

- *I now release any power I think my patterns may have over me.*

- *I now pattern my life after Jesus.*

*No one can make you feel inferior
without your consent.*

Eleanor Roosevelt

*If you make friends with yourself
you will never be alone.*

Maxwell Maltz

*A man who treasures his friends is
usually solid gold himself.*

Marjorie Holmes

*The strength you've insisted on assigning to
others is actually within yourself.*

Lisa Alther

Look In Your Mirror

D o you want to find out how you *really* feel about relationships, money, jobs and even God? All you have to do is look out into your world. Remember earlier when I talked about how we create the world we see and the experiences we have? Our minds are always creating, whether we are aware of it or not. And what we believe about ourselves, about money, about people and even about God, we will see reflected in our lives.

Using the world as a mirror is an excellent tool in getting in touch with our suppressed thoughts. Do you want to know how you really feel about money? Look at your checking account. Look at your savings account. Look at the clothes you wear. Is there lack? Is there fear? If there never seems to be enough, possibly you have the thought that there's never enough time, love or money to go around. If you have to work hard at a boring, demeaning job, possibly you may have the thought that life is hard and we can only earn love or money by the *sweat of our brow*.

Now, I'm not saying that having a lot of money is an indication of a high prosperity consciousness. I've known wealthy people who clung so desperately to their money, that there was no joy in the experience. Only fear and lack. What I am saying, though, is that there is a *feeling* that predominates your affairs. I've also known people who had little and were the happiest, richest people on earth. They had a high prosperity consciousness of the soul and it reflected out into their daily lives.

Do you want to know how you feel about relationships? Look at the relationships you currently have. I mean **all** of your relationships. That includes your work relationships, play relationships and even the brief relationship you may have with a waitress or a grocery clerk. Do you feel at ease with people or do you feel that you need to be hiding something? Are you afraid to look people in the eye, with love and acceptance, or do you expect the worst? Do you believe that "it's a jungle out there?" Do you think that people are always out for themselves, never caring for anybody else?

A few years ago, I reached a point of total burnout. I had been teaching some extensive and confrontational classes for over a year and the stress took effect. After my second class, I felt as if nobody cared for what I had to say. I felt as if I had nothing worth giving to the world. I felt drained, paranoid and afraid. What had happened was I had lost myself. I had become a TEACHER (the one who KNOWS everything, the one with ALL the answers) and lost the concept of being a teacher (one who teaches *and* learns with his students). The price for this stance was feeling burned out and sucked dry of all enthusiasm.

And it showed in my clientele. I couldn't get a client to work with me if I paid them! The truth is, I had lost my caring and compassion for people, and people felt it. I felt abandoned and lost. So I decided to give up my teaching and counseling career and return to the "real world." I decided to get a job in computer programming (my original profession). And so began a six-month period of really low self esteem. I had been out of the profession for six years and it seemed as if nobody wanted my services. I would go on interviews; some seemed promising, but nothing would shift. My wife was supporting us and I felt most of the time that I was a failure as a husband, as a man and as a human being.

But then I reflected on what was really going on. "What if," I thought, "this is how I **really** feel about myself all of the time?" Unworthy, useless, with no talents? And another thought entered my mind.

"This can be a time of growth for you, Jerry. This can be a golden opportunity to see whether you can love yourself, even though it looks to the world like you're a total failure. This is a time to see if you can let yourself feel and release all of that old low self esteem without believing that it's true."

So what I did was just *allow* those feelings to surface — to cry, to feel like a victim, to rant and rage at God. It wasn't easy. I felt many times that sooner or later my wife would wise up and leave me. But I trusted in the truth about myself. I trusted that there was a bigger meaning to all this. So I kept loving myself, even though I felt unlovable. I kept letting my wife love me, even though I felt unworthy. And I kept taking steps.

After about five months of fruitless job hunting, I decided I had to do something to create money. Anything was better than just sitting at home watching the bills pile up and waiting for calls. And then I remembered something I would tell my students. I would ask them,

"Can you love yourself, even if you were bagging groceries at Krogers?"

At that moment a small voice inside me said,

"Why don't you get a job bagging groceries at Krogers. Making $3.95 per hour is better than sitting at home making nothing per hour."

Something felt totally right about that thought. It felt like it was time for me to take my own acid test and see if I could still love myself. Trusting it, I went out the following day and applied for a temporary job at Krogers.

I remember the first day on the job, the shame and humiliation that wanted to well up and send me home. I remember looking at myself in the mirror — white shirt, black bow tie, maroon apron with a name tag — and thinking,

"What the hell am I doing here?"

But I decided to make the best of it and threw myself into the job. I decided to see what reflections I could create there. I began to play games with my mind. I would watch to see what kind of tip I would receive for carrying out groceries. And I found that when I was open, loving and accepting, people wanted me to carry out their groceries and would tip me. When I was angry, resentful and judgmental, I couldn't get anybody to accept my services. I began to watch my thoughts and feelings, I began to bless myself, my job and the people who came there. At night, Stav would come home and we would count the tips I created that day, and, even though it wasn't a fortune, it felt like one. On days that I was centered and loving, the tips were better.

And then a miracle began to happen. As I spent my time bagging groceries, I began to *notice* the people coming through the line — the silly, rowdy teenagers, the tired moms with little ones, the outrageous, loud construction workers, the quiet people, the demanding people, the loving people and the rude people. I started to care. I began to love once again the magic and wonder of this life of ours — the diversity and unity of love.

One day I was bagging the groceries for a Hindu couple when I noticed the woman's father was standing on the wrong side of the aisle. He was on **my** side, behind the checker. He was basically in the way and I felt a wave of irritation as I thought

"Foreigners! Always getting in the way!"

And then I *looked* at him. He was watching the checkout girl scan the articles and ring them up with a look of wonder on his face. He glanced at me and smiled and I smiled back. He just stood there, watching all that food go by. When I was finished packing the groceries, I handed the bag to him and again our eyes met. My heart opened.

"Welcome to America," I said.

He smiled and left with his daughter and son-in-law. A moment later, the woman returned and said to me, in that wonderful, flowing Indian accent,

"My father does not speak English — but he understood what you said."

I knew in that moment that my love for the world had returned and that the world was reflecting love back to me. A week later I had a job as a programmer and two weeks after that counseling clients began to call for my services. I've been successful at my job and counseling ever since.

When we are not afraid to look in the mirror, what we see looking back . . . is love.

Self Discovery Quiz

- *If there was something you were afraid to look at, inside yourself, what would it be?*

- *If you had a bullhorn attached to your head that blared out every thought you had, which thoughts would you be afraid that people would hear?*

- *What is your world reflecting to you today? Fear? Hate? Lack? Peace? Love? Joy?*

- *What is a characteristic that you judge about your relationship?*

- *What is a characteristic that you judge about your children?*

- *How can you begin to get love reflected back from the world?*

- *If you want to receive hugs from people in your life, how can you get those reflected?*

- *If you want to receive compliments and praise from people in your life, how can you get those reflected?*

It's smart to pick your friends —
but not to pieces.

Anonymous

A friend is a present you give yourself.

Robert Louis Stevenson

Don't ever question your wife's judgment;
after all, she married you.

Anonymous

We find comfort among those
who agree with us —
growth among those who don't.

Frank A. Clark

Relationships — The Intimate Mirror

When it comes to personal, intimate relationships, have you ever noticed how we always seem to create that *perfect* person who just seems to push our buttons no matter what? No matter how hard we try, we always end up with someone who knows not only which buttons to push, but also how hard to push and for how long to keep pushing. Why is that?

As mentioned earlier, I said that the world we see *out there* is merely an accurate reflection of what we think and believe inside our minds. We perceive what we think should be out there and then we attract the kind of people who will reinforce our beliefs. Anyone who does not match what we think and believe is unconsciously excluded from our realm.

When we get into a relationship, we are enrolled in an intimate course in personal development. Why? Because the person we attract will be the perfect person to teach us the lessons we need to learn at that given time. You see, what happens is that all relationships go through evolutionary stages. Unfortunately, many never grow past the initial growth stages into fruition.

All relationships start out as what *A Course in Miracles* calls a *special relationship*. A special relationship is a relationship where each partner sees the other person as having something that is lacking in themselves. At this point the relationship looks perfect because each person thinks that they are now "complete". This is the honeymoon stage of the relationship. Everything is peaches and cream, honey and granola. But what the ego considers a "marriage made in heaven," is really "a marriage made in hell" because a special relationship is actually based on guilt and fear. What we are secretly doing is putting all of our self esteem onto another person. We believe that they "complete us" and we are nothing without them. We begin to feel as if we would die if they left. And so, secretly, we hate and fear them because ultimately, they may leave. We are torn between the fear of desertion and our desire to love with all of our hearts. There is a saying that expresses accurately this stage:

"Love brings up everything unlike itself."

When we are in the presence of love, in the presence of acceptance, our Divinity begins to bring up all the little hurts and pains from the past. It wants to make us aware of the forgotten wounds that still need to be healed so that our life will be better. It wants us to realize that the past is over and that people are safe and we can trust again. It makes us think,

"Good! It's safe. Now I can cry. Now I can let my anger out. Now I can let go of my hurt around dad." Etc.

But our egos do not want us to heal. The ego believes that by being separate from one another, we are safe — that power lies in separation and isolation. It believes, "If you don't know what's going on with me, you can't change me and so I am in control." So when these old doubts, fears and anger begin to arise, the ego immediately clamps down and screams in our ear to shut down, put up those barriers!

And what we begin to do is, instead of looking at our issues, we begin to throw these thoughts and feelings onto our partner. Instead of looking at **our** wounds, we look at our partner's wounds. Instead of feeling our own low self esteem, we judge our partner.

"She's not that pretty. She could lose some weight."

"He doesn't make enough money."

"I hope people don't discover our age difference."

"He drives a dumpy car."

And so we start the age old game of judging the other person and making them wrong for all of *our* problems. We accuse them of not being open, when we secretly have no intention of really opening up our own secret hurts and fears. We may have the best intentions, but when it gets down to it, our fear usually wins out and we hold back our truth. Of course, they blame and judge us for the same things. From here, the pattern spirals downward into ultimately breaking up, or worse, staying together but shutting down all intimacy and love and having an empty relationship.

And we do it over and over again.

So how do we stop this merry-go-round? The Holy Spirit has an alternative to this marriage made in hell. It's called a *holy relationship*. A holy relationship is a relationship where both people acknowledge that they are already whole and complete. A holy relationship is based on trust, openness and love. There is no place for secrets in a holy relationship. At any time a special relationship can be transformed into a holy relationship once the participants are willing, but it does demand a shift in each of their minds. When a special relationship is changed into a holy relationship, the relationship will look very upsetting until both people begin to trust each other more and more. This is because the original goals have changed from secrecy to openness, from fear to love, from blaming to taking responsibility. Each person now has the opportunity to face the little hurts, monsters and fears, knowing that these thoughts are not the truth about them.

What my wife, Stav, and I do is remember that our partner *is* an accurate reflection of how we feel about ourselves. It may not be comfortable, but it is true. When Stav tells me something that I don't want to hear, I may resist at first (in fact, you can bet on it!), but once I settle down and I am willing to see what this part of my mind is saying, I find there is an element of truth in it. I may not agree with all she is saying, but there is a part that *does* strike home. What I have realized through the years is that it doesn't matter *what* is being said. What matters is that *my mind* somehow is attracting this message — either in an effort to change a condition or in an effort to feel a suppressed feeling. I have had many wonderful players in my life whose only function was to help me feel angry. Until I released those pent-up feelings, I continued to create people who pissed me off.

Remember, also, that your relationship reflects everything about you. This also means the good stuff. This also means that when times are wonderful and you are happy and she is happy, that this is a reflection of your mind too. *The love you see in your lover's eyes is merely your own love coming back to you.*

We are not crazy. We are not fools. We are children of God, more wonderful and powerful than we ever realized, and we want to remember this. Gaze into your mirrors to remember who you really are. If you are willing, you will see Christ.

Affirmations

- *The more I surrender to my relationship, the more I learn.*

- *It is safe to trust my husband/wife/lover.*

- *My relationship is cradled in the loving arms of God.*

- *It is safe to trust men.*

- *It is safe to trust women.*

- *Surrendering to my relationship is surrendering to God.*

- *Since the barriers I have to my relationship are the same barriers I have to God, I now see that my relationship is my path back to God.*

- *More and more I trust my reflections from my relationship.*

- *I cannot be hurt unless I want to be.*

- *My relationship never tells me anything about myself that I don't already think and feel deep inside.*

- *Whenever I get defensive, I am trying to ignore a suppressed thought I have about myself.*

Your health is bound to be affected if,
day by day,
you say the opposite of what you feel,
if you grovel before what you dislike,
and rejoice at what brings you
nothing but misfortune.

Boris Pasternak

The truth will set you free,
but first it's gonna piss you off!

Anonymous

The people to fear are not those
who disagree with you,
but those who disagree with you
and are too cowardly
to let you know.

Anonymous

It is important that you talk about your
feelings before they turn into something
destructive.

Tom Gallagher

The Truth Is . . .

There is a scene in the movie *Enemy Mine* that always touches me. It's a story about two enemies, an Earthman and a Drac — a reptilian life form, who are stranded on a hostile planet and are forced to learn to live together. At one point the Earthman is learning to read the Drac language from the alien's holy bible. He reads two passages aloud, in Drac, and then the Drac asks him to translate.

"Whenever one does harm to you, do not repay in kind. Love him instead."

The Earthman looks up.

"I've heard this before. On my planet"

"Of course," replies the Drac, "truth is truth."

"Truth is truth." What a wonderful affirmation of a universal concept. But sometimes our minds get stuck trying to find the truth. We've all heard the saying that truth is relative. That statement is true in **this** world, the world of perceptions. The world that I see and the world you see can be totally different. Take for example, two women involved in a wedding, the mother of the groom and the mother of the bride. After the wedding, we can interview them.

"Oh, it was absolutely horrible!" exclaims the mother of the groom. "Nothing went as planned. The ushers didn't know what to do, the flowers were late and we ran out of wine at the last minute. My ulcer is killing me. I'm glad it's over!"

The mother of the bride may have a different experience. "Oh, we had some problems, but all in all, it was a wonderful affair. We had to coach the ushers at the last minute, the flowers arrived after the ceremony, so we just put them on at the reception, and the wine ran out. One of our friends volunteered to run out and buy more and so we sipped soda and joked until it came. Oh, it was a challenge, but we survived. Besides, we still had fun."

The same incident, different interpretations. Whose interpretation is correct?

The same thing happens when we are having a fight with our relationship. We are convinced that our view is the only way to see it while our relationship is equally convinced that their side is right. What is the truth? The truth is that the issue is bigger then we realize and as *A Course in Miracles* states:

"You are never upset for the reason you think."

Remember that many times we create situations that remind us of something else, something from the past. And then we react with all that suppressed anger from the past.

So what is the Real Truth about us? The real truth is that we all are children of a loving, powerful, beautiful God and we have the opportunity to express that love at all times. That is what I call Truth with capital "T."

The truth (small "t") that we see every day, in this world, is variable, changing with people's perceptions. What you see is not the same as what I see. The problem arises when I try to convince you that my truth is more correct than your truth. And the more you resist my truth, the more angry I get and the more defensive you become.

Then there is the emotional truth. This is the truth of how we are feeling **in the moment.** Emotional truths are not based on logic or rationality. They can change in an instant, but in order for them to change, they **must** be expressed in some fashion. Such as:

"Yes, I am a child of God, but emotionally, right now, I feel totally unlovable."

"The truth for me, right now, is that I don't want to hear you and I want to be right about this."

"Right now, I feel as if I never want to forgive you. I'll do it when I'm good and ready!"

Many of us have a fear of expressing the emotional truth. We think that just because we feel *"I hate you and I never want to see you,"* that it literally means forever. So we hold back expressing our feelings. But emotional truths never last! All it means is that **right now**, I hate you and **right now** I feel like I don't want to see you again. Two minutes from now I may feel very different. In a relationship, we need to have the freedom to express these emotional truths without everybody reacting as if it were the end of the relationship. There are times when I want to be alone. There are times when I don't feel lovable. There are times when I don't feel loving towards my wife. It doesn't mean that these feelings are forever.

When we express the little truth first, ultimately it leaves room for the real Truth to be uncovered. The problem arises when we judge our little truths. We think they are so petty, so unspiritual, so mean. And yet, once they are expressed, once they are out in the open, they shrivel up in the light of love. Many times, after fighting a heated argument, Stav and I realize that the truth about the whole disagreement is that we were afraid and hurt. When we stop and tell the other person what we are afraid of happening, we realize that inside we are just little children, afraid that the love will go away. Once those issues are aired out, the love returns.

What I have learned, after numerous disagreements and broken friendships is to say:

"Lord, help me to see this through Your eyes, not mine."

Then I give myself permission to see and express my version of the truth, but also, I allow myself to shut up and listen to my partner's version of their truth. When I am willing to let go of my version of the truth and just allow another version in, my mind and heart expands. It does not mean that I have to give up my position. It just means that I am receptive to another idea. I may accept the new idea totally, I may reject it, or I may take part of it.

The truth is what is true for you in the moment. Tell yourself the truth, just as it is. Let yourself feel it and acknowledge it's truth *for you*. Then be willing to let the larger truth be revealed.

And just as many times we have to let the little truth out, there are times when the real Truth pops up, especially when it's least appreciated. Late one night Stav and I were having a crazy fight. We were totally furious with each other and hated each other. In a fit of one-upsmanship (I've been known to be pretty good at this), I stormed out of the house. I figured that since I didn't want to be home, I would go to the office and work through the night. And I wouldn't let her know where I was. Let her worry! Let her suffer! That'll teach her! But as I was leaving, Stav called out,

"Drive carefully!"

I was so mad! Even in our rage for each other the real Truth surfaced. At that moment she was a little saner than I was. She loved me, even as she hated me, and she still wanted me to be safe. I drove to work, fuming, sat at my desk and began to work. But my heart knew what I had to do. I called her, even though it was 12:30.

"I'm at work. I just didn't want you to worry."

"Thanks for calling. Why don't you come home now?"

"I'm still angry and upset. Anyway I'm already here, so I'll just work through the night."

"OK. I'll see you later," she said.

I worked for a few hours, but my heart wasn't in it anymore. The truth was, I missed her, I truly loved her and I didn't want to punish her. I came home, back to bed.

Though we still had our issues to handle, the real Truth of our relationship had surfaced. We loved each other and nothing was worth throwing that away. This helped in setting our issues into a different perspective.

Finally, I want to cover the thought that we have to be responsible for what we want to believe. One night, in one of my classes, a student asked,

"All these things that you are saying are so wonderful. But I was raised with different concepts. I was raised with sin and guilt and fear. How do I know which version is true?"

"Which version do you prefer to be true?" I asked.

I saw a light click in his eyes as he realized that **he** was the believer and he could chose whatever he wanted to believe. And he could change his mind - at any time.

"You have every right to believe anything you chose," I continued. "But which makes you feel closer to people? Fear or love? Which makes you feel closer to God? An angry, vengeful, old man or a forgiving Father?"

"The loving Father."

"Then believe in that."

There was a sense of peace on his face as he accepted that thought. The greatest gift that we can give ourselves is permission to believe in the good in ourselves, others and God. Trust that small, loving voice in your heart. It will never steer you wrong. That's because it never forgot the real Truth about you.

Self Discovery Quiz

- *Have you ever held back your truth from somebody? How did it feel?*

- *Have you ever seen somebody going down a destructive path and didn't say anything because it might rock the boat?*

- *Did you ever purposefully answer a question in such a way that the questioner got the wrong answer, even though you **knew** what they wanted you to say? Was that a lie or not?*

- *Is there somebody in your life that you feel isn't being totally honest? Who is it? What are you going to do about it?*

- *Do you have a hard time telling your relationship "I love you?"*

- *When you are angry, are you more interested in getting to the truth or winning the argument?*

- *Are there any past lies that have to be forgiven?*

It is the heart always that sees,
before the head can see.

Thomas Carlyle

Intuition is a spiritual faculty and
does not explain,
but simply points the way.

Florence Scovel Shinn

Spontaneity is only a term
for man's ignorance of the gods.

Samuel Butler

Listen to the voices.

William Faulkner

All you have to do is close your eyes
and wait for the symbols.

Tennessee Williams

A Sign From God

Wouldn't it be great if it were easy to talk to God? That all we had to do was ask a question and we would get an answer or a sign?

Well, I've got some good news and some bad news.

The good news is – God is *always* communicating with you and guiding you.

The bad news is – you're just not listening.

In the movie *The Man with Two Brains*, Steve Martin plays a recent widower who is falling in love with the sultry Katherine Turner. And he is torn between his loyalty and devotion to his dead wife and his feelings of lust for this new woman. And so he stands before a picture of his wife in the dining room and asks,

"I am torn between my love for you and my feelings for my new friend. What should I do? Should I go with her? Just give me a sign. Any sign."

It's quiet for a moment but then slowly there emanates from the picture a low voice.

"No . . . No . . . No . . ." it moans.

And then the lights begin to flicker and the picture shakes on the wall.

"No . . .No . . . NOOOO!!!" it continues.

And now the ground is shaking, the lights are flashing on and off and the French doors blow open as a hurricane force gale blows dust and leaves through the house, forcing Steve Martin to keep his balance.

"NO! ! NO! ! NOOOOO! !" the picture is wailing.

The wailing picture is spinning around and around on the wall as the winds assail Steve Martin. This keeps up for a few seconds and then the wind dies down, the picture stops spinning and the lights go back to normal. It ends with the picture moaning a plaintive,

"No . . . No . . .No . . ."

And Steve Martin says to the picture,
"Just any sign at all. I'll be waiting."
A Course in Miracles says,

The Holy Spirit's voice is as loud as your willingness to listen.

Text pg. 145 / 157

You see, God is talking to you all the time. Mostly though, we may not like hearing what we hear.

As you reach for something to eat that you know is not good for you, do you ever get a feeling, that says,

"You know you shouldn't eat that."

Have you ever heard a voice, in the middle of an argument that says,

"You know you're wrong. Why don't you just tell her and stop this insanity?"

Have you ever had the thought, as you were contemplating something dishonest,

"Don't do that. It's wrong!"

Have you ever had the thought, as you look at your wife,

"Tell her you love her."

That's God!

And how many times do we continue with what we want to do, regardless of the advice?

My friend Dave once told me about an incident he had with God. He had been angry for days because he had been praying for an answer to a question and God was mute. Finally, he had a temper tantrum with God. He started ranting and raving at God.

"I knew it! You're *not* really there for me! You don't care about my life or anything! I knew it all along!"

And then Dave got quiet, maybe from feeling guilty or just because he was psychically tired from his tirade. And a tiny, still Voice crept into his mind.

"I've been talking to you all the time. But you've already made up your mind and I can't get through!"

And Dave realized that he *had* made up his mind and that his mind had been shut to any other alternatives.

So the first thing to remember when asking for God's help is to have an open mind. Be open to possibilities and other options.

Sometimes people ask me,

"How can I tell whether the guidance I get is from God or from my ego?"

Well, when a good friend calls you on the phone, and you recognize her voice, how is it that you know it's her? Because you have an *ongoing* relationship. You know how she sounds, the phrases she uses, her various intonations. So too with hearing God's Voice. Develop a relationship with God. Get familiar with the Voice of God in you. Learn how it speaks to you and how it sounds. Many times you will find that it sounds just like your voice.

Also you will find that over time you can tell the ego's guidance because there is always a string attached. There is always some sort of secret agenda underneath the message. God's Voice is usually the first thought you get. It tends to be quiet, loving and certain. The ego's tends to be loud, persistent and bossy.

And don't wait for disaster to strike before asking for God's support. There is no problem or question too small for God so include Him in your daily life. Ask Him what you should eat for lunch. Ask Him which radio station should you listen to today. Ask Him which job should you do first. Get sensitive with this powerful aid, so that when times do get tough, you *know* how God's Voice always sounds to you.

Another way to help in distiguishing God's Voice versus the ego's is to call a person you trust for support. Remember to call somebody that you know will always tell you the truth, whether you like it or not. Sometimes, just talking to another friend has helped me to clear up my internal chatter and determine whether the guidance I am hearing is genuine or not.

If you are going to learn to trust the guidance you receive, you also need to trust that you will **never** be given the wrong guidance, even if it *seems* to be wrong. You do not need to know why you get the guidance you get. All you need to do is trust that God is always watching and protecting you. It is the commitment to *listening* and then *acting* that will help in making the inner voice clearer and louder.

My friend Marianne related a recent test of God's Voice. One night she was feeling desperately lonely and felt drawn to call her old boyfriend, which she *knew* would throw her into even deeper depression and negative feelings. But then she also had the thought to call me instead, to get some support. And so she posted a challenge to God.

"If the phone rings within two minutes, I'll call Jerry for support. If it rings in five minutes, I'll call my ex-boyfriend."

And then she waited. Two minutes passed without a sound. Just a few seconds after five minutes, though, the phone rang.

"So what did you do?" I asked.

"Well, I knew that *couldn't* be the right answer and so I didn't do anything."

"You wasted an answer from God?" I blurted out.

She was stunned by my response.

"But it was the wrong answer!!"

"How do you know?" I countered.

"Well, if I listened and called my boyfriend, I just would have felt worse later."

"And is that so bad? Maybe God wanted you to call. Maybe He knew that this time you would **finally** get tired of having your feelings jerked around! Maybe He knew you were ready to change."

As she sat in silence, thinking, a client in the next room, working with Stav, was venting a lot of anger into a pillow. She kept screaming over and over,

"Listen to meeee! Listen to meeeee! Listen to meeeee!"

Marianne looked at me.

"God's talking to you right now," I said. "In fact, He's screaming at you. He's trying to get through."

And we both burst out laughing.

"You know what I think you should do?" I said.

"What?"

"Well, I am not that powerful to get God to ring a phone for me. I usually get the K-Mart version of guidance. You know, intuition, feelings, a sense of what I should do. But for whatever reason, you can get a more obvious signal. So, what I think you should do is when you get home tonight, you pray to God and apologize for not listening and trusting Him. And then give yourself a vow that from now on, no matter what, if you ask for a sign and receive an answer, you will follow through – no matter what."

"But what if it's wrong?"

"If you think God would give you a wrong answer, why are you asking in the first place?"

"But what if it's from my ego?"

"Even if it's from your ego, what you will be demonstrating to the Universe is that you are now open and willing to *sensitize* yourself to guidance. And that you will now take full responsibility for any results you receive from following that guidance. Believe me, I trust that even if the guidance is wrong, and it is from your ego, God will step in and correct it. That is because you are now willing to trust at a higher level."

A few days later she called to tell me that she resisted asking God for any help because she was afraid of the answer. But then she trusted and she felt guided to take some time off from her work (an action I had been strongly supporting her in). Logic said that she needed the money and couldn't afford it. But she trusted anyway, spending the day puttering around the house and watching videos. The next day she received an unexpected check in the mail and also a new, lucrative contract in her job.

It takes discipline and courage to attune yourself to the Voice of God. Discipline in giving yourself the time to talk and listen to God. Courage to act on the instructions you receive. Sensitize yourself to the Voice of God. Sensitize yourself to the guidance all around you. You will find a wealth of good support, love and knowledge always available at your disposal.

You will find that you are never alone.

And **that** is a good sign!

Affirmations

- *I am always open to the guidance around me.*

- *God is always speaking to me and I love to listen.*

- *God has never failed me and She never will.*

- *I now trust that God will guide me throughout the day.*

- *I never lose when I listen to my inner Voice.*

- *It becomes easier and easier for me to determine my Divine Voice and my ego's voice. I cannot be fooled.*

- *There is no question to small to ask for help.*

On the Path Home

Issues arise as we make our way back to God. That's part of the human experience. But judging ourselves with these issues does not further our progress. It's necessary to learn to love and accept our human aspects. Many times we use our humanness to convince ourselves that we are not lovable, that we are indeed guilty and that we do not deserve love. Everybody does it and everybody suffers. I disagree with the saying,

"Fifty million Frenchmen can't be wrong."

Fifty million Frenchmen **can**, and have been, wrong!

All the things I really like to do are either immoral, illegal or fattening.

Alexander Woollcott

You can't expect to hit the jackpot if you don't put a few nickels in the machine.

Flip Wilson

The great composer does not set to work because he is inspired, but becomes inspired because he is working.
Beethoven, Wagner, Bach and Mozart settled down day after day to the job in hand with as much regularity as an accountant settles down each day to his figures.
They didn't waste time waiting for inspiration.

Ernest Newman

Coping with Igor

Sometimes I get a client who wants to work on his issues with his ego. I remember one who told me how he wanted to hold his ego up to God's light and burn it out of him. I felt sad.

A Course in Miracles states many times that we need to learn to love our creations. The ego, a misguided thought system based totally on fear and separation, is **our** creation. God didn't make it. The world doesn't force it on us. It's our misguided thought. Nobody else's. Notice, though, the Course says to love our creations just as God loves His creations. It doesn't say to believe in them. Ever notice how when we are in our ego, how fearful everything looks? We're suspicious of every action, we question every motive and wait for when the other shoe's going to drop. This is a decision that we make. We are **deciding** to believe that we will be hurt, that people are out to get us — that there isn't enough time, love or money to go around.

The ego is like a fearful child who is trying to run the world and knows deep inside that it is not qualified. The ego knows that there is another part of us (our Divine part) that does not believe in fear, in lack, in limitation. The ego feels "snubbed" because the Divine part does not acknowledge it's existence — an existence based on fear and separation. And so the ego uses tools like denial, attack, projection and fear to stay in control. Imagine being only four years old and being chairman of the board of General Motors. Being a child and in an area obviously over your head, you may react with fear. You may try to control others, make them do what you want them to do through fear.

"I don't like you. You're fired! I want it my way!"

What would happen, though, if we decided to love the ego as our misguided child — a child in fear? What would happen if we took the ego's little hand (remember, it's our creation) and led it to a sandbox?

"Look, it's OK. It's safe. You're not going to be hurt. Would you like to play in this sandbox instead? Here's a pail and a shovel and a truck."

What would happen if, instead of cowering at the fears the ego projects, we simply listened, let it be heard and acknowledged,

"Thank you for sharing?"

Through years of practice and acceptance, I have learned to accept my ego, to listen to it but not be guided by it. To let it have its temper tantrums and not be afraid of that mouse squeaking at the world.

I have learned to gently laugh at my ego. In the movie *Young Frankenstein*, I love the role of Igor — Frankenstein's assistant. When they first meet, Frankenstein sees that Igor has a hump on his back.

"You know, I'm a pretty good surgeon," says Frankenstein. "I can remove that hump of yours."

Igor looks at Frankenstein, innocently.

"What hump?" he asks, without blinking an eye.

"That hump," points Frankenstein.

Igor continues to stare at Frankenstein as if he were crazy. Frankenstein starts to say something, stammers under that stare, and finally gives up.

"Oh, never mind."

Later in the movie, the hump is on Igor's *other* shoulder, and Frankenstein notices it.

"Wasn't your hump . . . on the other . . . side . . . ?"

Frankenstein sees the look in Igor's eyes and again gives up.

"Oh, never mind!"

I call my ego my Igor. Whenever I want to confront those unlikeable parts of myself, my ego stares me down and says,

"What hump? What anger? I'm not angry. What fear? I'm not fearful. Everybody else is fearful, but not me."

Learning to love every part of yourself is a process of acceptance, it's a process of accepting all your aspects, humps and all. It's a process of trust and a process of laughter. Learn to laugh gently at your mistakes. Laugh gently at your blind spots. When we learn to love and accept ourselves, then so does the world. As Antoine de Exupéry said,

"Angels can fly because they take themselves lightly."

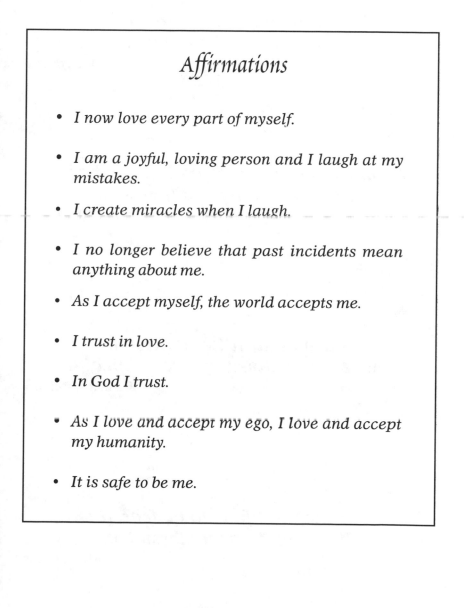

Affirmations

- *I now love every part of myself.*

- *I am a joyful, loving person and I laugh at my mistakes.*

- *I create miracles when I laugh.*

- *I no longer believe that past incidents mean anything about me.*

- *As I accept myself, the world accepts me.*

- *I trust in love.*

- *In God I trust.*

- *As I love and accept my ego, I love and accept my humanity.*

- *It is safe to be me.*

*Better face danger once
than always be in fear.*

Anonymous

*We must not let our fears hold us back
from pursuing our hopes.*

John F. Kennedy

*Fear is that little darkroom
where negatives are developed.*

Micheal Pritchard

*Nothing in life is to be feared.
It is only to be understood.*

Marie Curie

Who's Afraid of the Big Bad...

A *Course in Miracles* teaches that there are only two emotions — love and fear. Love was created by God and is eternal and unchanging. Fear was created by man. What is fear? Very simply, fear is the absence of love. Fear is the state of denying the love that is around us and acting as if we are alone. When we created the ego, we thought that somehow we had separated ourselves from God. We thought that somehow we hurt God, we overthrew Him and took possession of the universe. None of these thoughts are true. But in a wave of fear that God would punish us, we closed our spiritual eyes to God and waited for His awesome retribution. And from that original thought (original sin), we made the world, the pain, the war, and the fear.

Every day we see our fear in the uncertainty of the economy, the jealousies in our relationships, the fear of having our secret thoughts exposed, the fear of not being able to pay the rent, etc. But we have become so accustomed to being in fear that most of us do not even know we are living in it. We don't realize that we are living lives of *quiet desperation*.

Men especially have a hard time acknowledging the fear that is running their lives. We have been brought up for so long to be the pioneer, the challenger, the barbarian, that we suppress the true feeling that is driving us. We may *act* brave in some areas, but in areas of the heart, the fear drives us wild. We are afraid that being vulnerable and caring will make us look weak and so we put on a strong, unemotional front, thereby wrecking the very relationships we hold dear. And that, of course, brings up even more fear.

From fear arise all of the other negative emotions. Anger is fearful attack of possible future hurts. Greed is fear of not having enough money or possessions. Jealousy is fear of not enough love. Alcohol and drug addictions are fears of low self esteem and inadequacy.

I've heard a few acronyms for fear that really apply. One is **F**alse **E**vidence **A**ppearing **R**eal. Another good one is **F**eelings **E**xperienced **A**s **R**eal. Or as my friend John Hukill says, **F**orget **E**verything **A**nd **R**un. You see, fear is not the enemy. It is merely a feeling, an illusion. But when we make decisions based on our fear, then we make it real.

For example, you see a person that you feel attracted to. You want to ask them out for a date, but the instant you dial the phone or begin to walk up to them, you freeze. All those thoughts of "I'm not good enough," "She'll laugh in my face" or "Why would she want to be with me?" flood your mind and you stop. You hang up the phone in terror or walk past her as if you didn't care. That is an example of making our fear real. Now not only is the fear in our mind, now it's out in the world, and it's keeping us from experiencing the full range of life. There is just as much that we can learn from a "no" as from a "yes." She may want to date you, but she too, may be in fear. Someone has to take the first step!

In *A Course in Miracles*, Jesus says that He cannot take away our fear. When we ask Him or God to take away our fear, we are implying that we are not responsible for it. He further says that God would not interfere with our fear because to do so would go against a basic right that He gave us — our free will. To overthrow our right to be fearful would not be loving. Rather, we should ask for help in removing the cause of our fear. We should ask for help in healing any separation we may feel between ourselves and God, or ourselves and others. We need to remember that fear is a choice, not something that is **thrust** upon us.

When I would find myself in paralyzing fear, my teacher, Joe Heaney, would support me in going home, getting into bed, pulling the covers over my head and letting my fears have a field day. I would let every fearful thought come to mind, let myself shake with terror and imagine every horrible thing that could happen to me. What I would find is that after about fifteen minutes I would get tired of being afraid and the fear got smaller. It actually took more energy to keep the fear going than to take *any* step towards my goals.

Our egos use fear as a way of holding back our love but they never allow us to see how deeply our fear goes. Because if we did,

we would soon stop listening to the ego. So in order to s.
control, our egos only allow us to have a little taste of fear a.
time. Our egos allow us to feel "apprehensive" or "anxious", but
never downright fearful. It's like living down the street from an
offensive garbage dump. Now and then we get a whiff of what's
going on, but never enough to actually make us want to change. In
this way the ego can effectively disempower us without our realizing what is happening. But when we give ourselves a "fear break"
and really let the fears run wild, we see how draining this emotion
is and, hopefully, this gets us into action.

The movie *Defending Your Life* is all about fear. What I love
about the movie is that it is very funny and yet has a deep spiritual
message. According to the movie, when we die, we go to a place
where we review our lives to determine whether we have overcome
enough of our fear to go on to the next plane of existence, or to return
back to Earth for another chance.

Albert Brooks plays a somewhat, successful businessman, who
never totally went for his dream — fear held him back. Meryl Streep
plays a housewife, who, in her own way, lived life to her fullest. Their
differences in character show up in a restaurant scene. They are both
served immense dinners and begin to dig in. Meryl is enjoying her
spaghetti and slurping it up, strand by strand. Suddenly Albert sees
his prosecutor sitting at a table across the room and instantly goes
into fear. He's afraid his prosecutor will judge the size of his meal and
think that he is a pig. He's afraid of what his prosecutor will think. He
tries to get Meryl to stop eating her food like a child. She giggles and
continues anyway, while he continues to try to get her to "act like an
adult". Of course his appetite is ruined and the meal isn't enjoyed.

Fear keeps us from being in the moment. It keeps us from
living life from joy and aliveness. Fear is that voice that constantly
reminds us that if we are not good, we will be punished or embar-
rassed. Fear is what keeps us from skipping down the street in joy,
laughing out loud, crying without shame. Fear is the mind killer.
Fear is the life killer.

So what do we do with this thing called fear? Susan Jeffers
has an answer. She wrote a book entitled *Feel the Fear and Do It
Anyway*. It is a wonderful book about living with this feeling called
fear. It's not about beating fear but it's about acknowledging when

then taking the next step anyway. The book is
t exercises and examples.

, writing this book has brought up waves of fear
tly had to look at my own feelings of low self
esteem, past failures and false pride. Fear silenced many of my
words — for a while. The only thing I did know to do was to write
something **every day** — *no matter how I felt*. I would run through
my mind what was the worst that could happen to me if I wrote this
book. And then I would list the gifts I would receive by extending
my love in this manner. At first it took time to list my fears and
benefits but after the first few times, it became automatic and now
I just sit down and write, fearful or not, low self esteem or not,
angry or not.

And in taking each step you develop courage, you develop an
experience that the fear that seemed so real is not real. There is a
scene in the movie *Three Kings* in which George Clooney is supporting a soldier who has some fear about going into battle. He
tells the man,

"The way this works is, you do the thing you're scared shitless
of and you get the courage *after* you do it – not before you do it."

"That's a dumb ass way for it to work," replies the soldier. "It
should be the other way around."

"I know – but that's the way it works."

Remember, we cannot tell the difference between fear and
excitement. We all have a fear of falling, but most of us love the
excitement of a roller coaster, flying down a hill. Our bodies actually cannot tell the difference. The physiological responses are the
same. So turn your fear into excitement. Let yourself get excited
about asking a person for a date, get excited about getting that new
job or career, get excited about painting, writing or sculpting. Get
excited about life.

So let's propose a new acronym for fear — **F**eeling **E**xcited
And **R**eady.

Self Discovery Quiz

- *Is there something that you secretly want to do but you're afraid of failing?*

- *Is there something that you secretly want to do but you're afraid of succeeding?*

- *Think of a situation that you feel fearful about. Ask yourself, "If I knew what I really wanted out of this situation, what would be my next step?"*

- *How would Jesus handle fear in taking any new step?*

- *Is there something that you are afraid to tell your relationship? Your children? Your boss?*

- *If you had no fear, what would your relationship look like?*

- *If you had no fear, who would you date?*

- *If you had no fear, where would you work?*

- *If you had no fear, would you paint pictures? Write a book? Write poetry? Open a cafe? Say "I love you" more?*

- *Is God a fearful God or a loving God?*

- *Does God want you to be afraid of Him?*

- *If you were on your death bed right now, what would you regret not having done? When will you do it?*

*Many a man's profanity
has saved him from
a nervous breakdown.*

Anonymous

*Those who love deeply never grow old;
they may die of old age,
but they die young.*

Arthur Wing Pinero

*The worst sin toward our fellow creatures
is not to hate them
but to be indifferent to them;
that's the essence of inhumanity.*

George Bernard Shaw

*When you give vent to your feelings,
anger leaves you.*

Jewish proverb

Feel to Heal

Have you ever been in the presence of somebody who is telling you how *great* things are in their life, but when you walk away, your gut tells you that they're not being totally honest? Have you ever been with someone who *acts* confident and self assured but deep inside, you know it's just an act? Conversely, have you ever been in the presence of somebody whose life seems to be falling apart, and yet you feel a sense of peace and love?

Whether we are aware of it or not, we all feel. Being human is a feeling experience, but most of us have learned not to listen to our feelings, to ignore them. Why? Because feelings are not always comfortable. Feelings are not rational. They don't fit neatly in an intellectual world. In some families, feelings are ignored or shamed out of us. Feelings sometimes tell us things that contradict what the world is telling us, like when somebody is telling us what we **want** to hear, but we know deep inside it's not the truth.

Feelings do not just go away. Unexpressed feelings are like unsent letters. Until they are addressed and delivered, they just pile up and clutter your life. If there is a feeling that you have resistance in expressing, Life will send people in our world who will activate that suppressed feeling. And the more we try to suppress it, the more Life tries to help. And so we may turn to physical ways — eating too much, drinking, smoking, sex or drugs in an effort to silence that quiet, insistent voice inside or to escape the feelings of a painful childhood. And the more we persist in **not** expressing the feeling, the more we develop character defects — ways of acting, that try to compensate for the feeling that needs to be expressed.

All character defects stem from a suppressed feeling. Low self esteem spawns off such defects as perfectionism, egotism, pride and bullying behavior. Suppressed anger gives birth to aggressive behavior, control and manipulation and being judgmental. Guilt

creates blaming others, unforgiveness, revenge and self righteousness. And fear — the mother of negative feelings — spawns *reacting*
to life with attack, greed and lack, instead of responding with love.
This is just a small example of the ways we suppress our feelings.

For example, when we feel insecure, we will look to the world
to somehow verify and acknowledge us. If I have a feeling of low
self esteem and do not address it, I will look to the world to tell me
how great I am. I will manipulate and control in order to get into a
position to be complimented and affirmed. I will try to get people
to compliment and acknowledge me. When I am acknowledged,
I'll feel great. When I'm not, I'll feel like a failure. But the love
from out there will never be enough. You see, the feeling of insecu-
rity is *in me* and no amount of love, hugs and compliments from
out there will ever fill that black hole inside. And so I continue
looking for love in all the wrong places, working harder, striving
harder, and creating more stress.

What can we do about these feelings? The first step is to
acknowledge the feeling that is coming up, without judging yourself for having the feeling. If you are feeling angry, tell yourself the
truth: "I am angry!" Don't try to sugar coat the feeling — that in
itself is another way of intellectualizing the feeling.

When I am working with someone who wants to open to their
feelings, I try to get them to boil down the feeling to its basic
essence. I usually support them in only using six feelings — joyful,
angry, sad, numb, fearful and guilty. There is an American Indian
saying, "When you name the beast, you own it." When a person
begins to name the beasts that have been running their life, then
they become conscious of the ways they are acting and from there,
they can change — if they want to. So I limit my client to just those
six feelings. For example, if you are feeling *irritated* — that's a form
of anger. Feeling *apprehensive* is a form of fear. *Frustration* is a
form of anger. Feeling *paranoid* is a form of fear. Being *not aware
of anything* is numb. Feeling *happy* or *content* is joyful. Feeling *blue*
is sadness. And feeling *depressed* is suppressed anger.

After a couple of days of logging the current feeling every
hour, a client can begin to identify the predominant feeling running through their life. It's surprising and sad how many times the
word "numb" appears. But that in itself is a wake-up call. As they

become aware of the numbness, they become aware of the times they become numb and then can identify the feeling that they're **really** trying to suppress.

Another way to get in touch with feelings is to check how your body is feeling. Suppressed emotions will manifest in many ways on your body. For example, the stomach is usually associated with anger or power — the solar plexus with guilt, fear or will power — the heart with sadness or joy. If you find your stomach churning throughout the day, you may want to ask yourself if there is some unresolved anger floating around. These emotions can also show up as diseases or physical conditions. A good resource for helping to determine the suppressed thoughts and feelings for any disease is Louise Hay's book *You Can Heal Your Life*. In it she lists most of the common ailments, their corresponding emotions and an affirmation.

When I was taking my Six-Month Program, Joe, my teacher, was always asking me how I felt, or how my body felt. It seemed like I could never give the right answer. I would say I was feeling fine, and my classmates would retort that I was suppressing something. And so I would pick a feeling I thought I was feeling. And of course, this was usually wrong too. If I thought I was sad, I was told I was angry. If I thought I was angry, I was told I was sad. If I thought I was feeling peaceful, I was told I was fearful. Crazy!

I constantly felt blindsided by this strange concept of feeling my feelings. Though I knew that there was a purpose in feeling all this stuff, I just couldn't see any advantage in doing it. What I didn't know at the time was that I was always choosing to share the feeling that I felt *safe* feeling. To actually state truthfully that I was angry when I was really feeling angry scared me. To actually acknowledge my sadness or fear when I was really feeling sadness or fear would make me seem weak and fragile, or so I thought. As far as I was concerned, the more I could let myself feel, the worse I would feel.

I remember once asking Joe, just before the Program,

"Will the Program help me feel better?"

"Oh definitely," he replied. "You'll feel *much* better. You'll feel ALL of your feelings better. You'll feel your anger better, you'll feel your hate better and you'll feel your love better."

And so I persevered through the trainings. I didn't know it, but what Joe was trying to teach us was that as we allowed ourselves to experience and express our emotions, we would actually feel more alive. Many times he would tell me,

"Jerry, you're sitting on all your aliveness! You're sitting on all your power. When are you going to let it out?"

Well, a few months later, I got a taste of how it feels to *let it out*. The community was hosting a country-western dance and we were all supposed to dress up in country-western gear. You know, jeans, boots, cowboys hats. Well, I *hated* country-western gear and I felt a lot of resentment around having to spend money on clothes that I would probably never wear again. I was sitting at my desk at work, fuming, when I asked myself,

"Well, if I could have it my way, how would I *want* to dress."

And I suddenly had this flash of Clint Eastwood as the High Plains Drifter. I felt this daredevil rush of excitement as I imagined showing up at the dance dressed like that. Then my ego kicked in.

"You can't do that! What will everybody think? You're supposed to get dressed in jeans and boots."

But the more I felt it, the more excited I got. And so I went to a costume shop and rented a black, flat-brimmed hat, the long, black coat, black pants and a white shirt. You know what? When I put it on, I felt like a million bucks!

So, even though I was still a little apprehensive, I showed up at the hoe-down dressed like Clint Eastwood. When Joe saw me, his eyes widened and his face broke into a wide grin.

"That's you!" he exclaimed. "That's what you've been hiding! There's a gangster, a scoundrel in you – and I love it!"

It was great! I felt so alive that night, letting this secret part of me out. I ended up dancing just about every dance. I learned a lesson that night that following your heart, even if it goes against other people's wishes, will always bring you joy. From then on, I began to experiment more and more with telling my truth as I saw it and expressing my wishes, whether they were right or wrong. And like Pinocchio, I transformed from a wooden, unfeeling puppet to a real live person.

As you get better at identifying your feelings, hopefully you will get professional help at resolving the original issues that started those feelings. It is very important as we travel the road back to God, that we see that we are not alone, that we are not the only people with these thoughts and feelings, that others can guide us from their lessons. Private counseling, group therapy or workshops will help.

Learn how to handle anger. Learn how to release grief. Learn how to face your fear. Learn how to handle success. My personal preference is working with a counselor who is familiar with Breath Integration. I have found it to be particularly helpful in releasing emotions linked to past trauma, such as alcoholism, child abuse, incest, ridicule in school, etc. But whichever form of therapy you choose, it will be the right one for you. Trust yourself in this. I have seen many people try different methods of therapy and grow from each one. If you want to heal and are open to learning, you cannot keep healing away.

Finally, as you become more acquainted with your emotions, remember to love yourself all the time. It is important not to identify with the feelings; just acknowledge that they are there and take appropriate action. There is a big difference between the statements,

"I *am* guilty for such and such" and "I *feel* guilty for such and such."

The first one identifies **you**, the second identifies a feeling that you have. When you are feeling guilty, make amends if someone else is involved and then do something nice for yourself, while you feel the guilt. When I wrecked my car a few years ago, my friend Phil supported me to love myself as much as I could and to take my wife out that night for a nice candlelight dinner with wine and to have a nice dessert afterwards. In other words, to love myself regardless. The ego, who always expects punishment, goes crazy at times like this. When you are feeling sad, ask for a hug or reassurance, while you are feeling sad. No longer use your feelings as a way to isolate yourself from love, especially from your own love.

When you begin to see that feelings are a wonderful tool for interacting with the world and expressing your true power, you will become more at ease. You'll become more YOU. It's the quickest way back home.

Affirmations

- *I now open up to the feeling side of my divinity.*

- *The more I feel, the more I heal.*

- *Every day it gets easier for me to express my feelings.*

- *I always express my feelings responsibly and safely.*

- *I am now in touch with the alive and feeling nature of God within.*

- *I learn from my feelings.*

- *I now listen to the messages my body is sending me.*

- *My feelings are my key to Heaven.*

- *My feelings make it even easier for me to create the life I desire.*

A person who talks about his inferiors hasn't any.

Anonymous

Judging others is a dangerous thing; not so much because you may make mistakes about them but because you may be revealing the truth about you.

Anonymous

Your opinion of others is apt to be your opinion of you.

B. C. Forbes

Do not judge, and you will never be mistaken.

Jean Jacques Rousseau

Do not condemn the judgment of another because it differs from your own. You may both be wrong.

Dandemis

Here Comes the Judge

When we are in fear, one of the tools that the ego uses in order to keep us from realizing that we are in fear is to judge. What is judgment? Judgment is comparing yourself with others and deeming either them, or yourself, to be lacking. Judgment always comes from a place of low self esteem. It's an attempt to put others below us, so that we can feel better than they. Or it's an attempt to put ourselves lower than others, so that we don't even have to try to be better. Either way, it's an effort to throw off feelings in an attempt not to look at them.

When I see an aspect of myself that I do not like, what my ego wants me to do is to throw off that aspect onto somebody else — make *them* unlovable. Judge *them* for the same qualities I dislike about myself, but make believe it's **all** in them. Judgments keep us safe — or so we think. Safe to continue living our lives in a private hell, surrounded by "idiots" and "sinners." Safe from ever having to feel the fear or pain of looking within. Safe from opening to love.

When I find myself judging others, I now ask myself,

"What part of myself acts the same way as this person? What part has the same qualities that I dislike in myself?"

Now, don't get stuck in looking only at the act. For example, if you have judgments about alcoholics or drug users and you never touch the stuff, you may be tempted to think that this is not a reflection of yourself. But ask yourself honestly,

"In what ways am I addicted? How do I suppress my feelings?"

You may get answers such as you smoke too much, eat too much or depend on sex too much to get gratification. Maybe your addiction is not committing — flitting from one relationship to another in an effort to never feel hurt. Maybe your addiction is working long hours in an attempt to prove your worth. Many of us, myself included, use television as a way to numb out and go unconscious. I believe that we are all addicts to some degree because we are all afraid to feel our feelings. It's just that some of these addictions are more socially acceptable than others.

Now I am not saying that we need to stop eating, smoking, having sex or watching TV. These are all enjoyable pastimes that add to the joy of life. But is there an area where you know, deep inside, you're doing a little too much? When you are upset, do you find yourself reaching for a donut or lighting up a cigarette? Do you flick on the TV when your wife wants to talk? Do you bury yourself deeper in the newspaper when your children want attention?

So when you find yourself judging another person, be willing to check inside for the originator of the judgment. When I am feeling low self esteem, or even loathing at my body, I will tend to judge other bodies. I will see people as too fat, too skinny, too ugly, too beautiful, too short or too tall. Until I take my judgment back, until I acknowledge that I am the one with the problem, I will continue to see fat, ugly, short, tall people. But judgment exacts a strict price. You see, when you persist in judging others, the divine part of you knows that you are only hurting yourself, and so you will subconsciously try to heal the separation. Over time, if the judgment is not released, you will end up living out your own judgments.

If you are a parent, you'll probably be able to relate to my next example. Remember when you were growing up? Remember the judgments you had on how your parents raised you? Did you ever see your parents do something that you thought was mean and cruel and tell yourself,

"When I grow up, I'll never be like that!"?

Later in life you became a parent. And did you ever find yourself doing exactly the same thing to your child and suddenly realizing,

"My God! I'm acting just like my dad!"?

At this point, most of us judge ourselves for being like our parents. But there is a larger lesson. I remember a time when my daughter was two and she was being particularly whiny one day. Her mother was in the hospital for major surgery and it felt like my world was falling apart. Mary Jean kept hanging on me and whining and complaining. I couldn't stand it anymore and I suddenly lost my temper. I remember screaming at that little girl to **"SHUT UP!"** Mary Jean crumbled to the floor in tears and a moment later I joined her, crying also. I felt so bad, so guilty, and I thought,

"I'm just as bad as my mom."

It took me years to realize that my mom wasn't bad, but she too, had bad days. She too felt overwhelmed with problems, resentful at being a parent, and worried about the future. When I yelled at Mary Jean, I was crazy and I finally had an inkling of how my mom sometimes felt with me. The lesson here is not to judge ourselves for becoming just like our parents. The lesson is to have some compassion, to see our parent's side, to see how they felt. And when I found it in my heart to forgive myself for losing my temper, I also found myself forgiving my mother.

There is a divine part of us that KNOWS that our parents were human and it wants us to see our parents in a different light — with compassion. Our Divine Self knows that as long as we are judging another person we are being separate and unloving. The truth about us is that we are all inherently loving, compassionate beings because we are of God. So we try to find a way to heal the separation by trying to see through another's eyes. If we don't let go of the judgments through forgiveness or compassion, then we end up acting them out, in an effort to realize how the other person felt.

In one of my relationships I used to judge my girlfriend for being inept when it came to handling her checkbook. She was always bouncing checks or forgetting to log an entry and this made me feel as if I were better than her. I felt she was a financial flake. A few months after we broke up, I was discovering new areas of my life that I didn't want to explore and I found myself in a morass of feelings. I didn't know which end was up. And of course, one day, I made an error in my checkbook. In one month I ran up over $250 in bounced check fees alone, before I corrected the error. I felt inept. I felt stupid. I felt — like a financial flake. When I finally got back into my right mind, I actually laughed. My judgments had come home to roost (or roast). I got to live out my judgments of my girlfriend and in the process I learned to have some compassion for her and for myself.

A Course in Miracles asks,

Remember how many times you thought you knew all the 'facts' you needed for judgment, and how wrong you were! Is there anyone who has not had this experience? Would you know how many times you merely thought you were right, without ever realizing you were wrong?

Teacher's Manual pg. 26 / 27

How many people have we judged, and still judge, without seeing their side, and never finding out how wrong we are? How many opportunities for love do we want to pass up before we let go of this misguided tool?

And how many people do we judge not worthy of our love and thereby miss out on an opportunity for a new experience? Every week my wife and I tithe a percentage of our income back to God. We donate to our church, institutions or people who teach or demonstrate what we want to learn. Generally we just write out the check and send it on its way. But just writing out a check denies us the actual **feeling** of giving. So one week we decided to take out about $30 in five dollar bills and physically give them away to people who we felt drawn to give.

I was coming home from work one afternoon, when up ahead, at the stoplight, I saw a homeless person, with a sign asking for money for food. I took out a five dollar bill and waited for him to reach me. Before he got to me, he crossed in front of my car and went to the van on my right. He was scruffy, unshaven and dirty and he had a slightly arrogant and angry look, as if he **expected** people to give to him. His hand was extended with an attitude of,

"Well? Are you going to give to me or not?"

I immediately changed my mind, thinking, "I don't want to give to *him*. He wouldn't even appreciate it" and I crumpled the bill in my hand.

And then the lesson for the day from the *Course* floated across my mind - *"Only my condemnation injures me."*

I realized I was condemning this man. I was judging him unworthy of my gift, because he didn't look right, act right and because he may not even feel grateful. And I realized that I was also condemning myself to those same judgements. I thought,

"Do I want to make my judgements real? Do I want to see myself the same way?"

As he came around the back of the car and up my side, I rolled the window down and handed him the bill. He looked at me with these gentle, loving eyes and said,

"Thank you. . . and bless you."

Love had been there all the time – I just didn't want to see it. And I felt my heart swell as I realized that I no longer wanted to condemn him or myself. Holding back my gift would have only hurt me.

Who needed that gift? Not him, but me.

Jesus told us,

"Judge not, lest ye be judged."

Judgments always come home to their maker.

How does it feel to let go of judgments? When you are in a place of peace, of non-judgment, you no longer feel threatened by the world *out there*. Have you ever had a day where you were on top of the world? You felt great, powerful and loving. It didn't matter if the traffic was slow — you just enjoyed yourself anyway. It didn't matter if you were overweight, you just accepted yourself. You felt close to God. You felt close to yourself. You felt close to people. It didn't matter how they looked or even acted. You just accepted. Remember that feeling? That is peace. How does it feel to let go of judgments? It feels great!

Affirmations

- *I now take back every unloving thought that I have held towards others.*

- *I now take back every unloving thought that I have held towards myself.*

- *I now love myself.*

- *I now forgive myself for being judgmental.*

- *I no longer need my judgments to feel safe. I am already safe.*

- *The more I accept others, the more I am accepted by others.*

- *I now allow myself to have my process.*

- *I now allow others to have their process.*

- *Nothing can change the truth about my divinity. I am a child of God.*

One day a warrior was walking through the crowded bazaar in the city of Basra, when suddenly he saw Death among the crowds, looking at him. And Death had a surprised, astonished look on it's face.

The man panicked and in his fear he suddenly had a thought,

"I have the fastest horse in all of Arabia. If I can get away from Him and escape to the mosque in Damascus by noon tomorrow, I'll be safe."

Now Damascus was many, many miles away, and nobody had ever covered that distance in one day. Nevertheless, he took off, riding all the rest of the day and throughout the night. He arrived shortly before noon, tired and hungry, but feeling safe and secure. But as he got off his horse, he turned around and saw Death standing there, waiting.

"I was amazed to see you in Basra yesterday," said Death in a gravelly voice. "I knew we had an appointment to meet today at noon in Damascus and I didn't think you'd be here on time."

An Arabian tale

You Can Run,
But You Cannot Hide

Have you ever actually found a geographical cure to your problems? ie "My life will get better if I move to Colorado." Have you ever met anybody who actually fixed their relationship issues by getting a new girlfriend or wife?

Have you ever known anybody who has successfully run away from the lessons in their life?

I don't know about you, but I have never been able to run away from my lessons. They follow me around. Well, there is a reason for this. As *A Course in Miracles* says,

> *Free will does not mean that you can establish the curriculum. It means only that you can elect what you want to take at a given time.*

Text - Introduction

In other words, there are certain lessons that you are bound to learn, whether you like it or not. The only question is *when* will you decide to learn them?

And so, lessons are presented to us, over and over, until they are finally learned. And if they aren't learned, well, they're presented again. For example, check in and see if you know of anybody that these scenarios pertain to.

- An intellectual person who is constantly confronted with emotional issues in an effort to get him to feel.

- A controlling person confronted with situations that are out of control in an effort to help this person release their need to control.

- A person, afraid of being lonely, who cannot create a relationship in an effort to get them to love themselves, regardless if they are in a relationship or not.

In the movie *Misunderstood*, Gene Hackman plays the father of two boys, whose mother dies from a lingering disease while the boys are visiting relatives. When the boys come home, they ask for their mother but the father tells them that she's away, visiting. Andrew, the older son sees through the lie and confronts his father. The father tells Andrew the truth and then asks him not to tell his brother for fear that the news will further weaken his younger brother's delicate constitution.

What this sets in motion, though, is that the son is not allowed to express his own feelings. He has to stuff them down. He begins to hang around cemeteries and he watches other people's funerals so that in this little way he can cry and feel some release. Later, the truth comes out and the younger son learns of his mom's death but the father still does not show any emotion. The father stuffs his emotions, like a man, and expects Andrew to do the same.

The older son then, in order to prove that he is brave and a grown up, begins playing a dangerous game. The movie ends up with Andrew, seriously hurt, lying in his father's arms, finally getting the love and attention he needed all along.

And Gene Hackman's heart *finally* cracks as he begins to let all those suppressed feelings out. He finally sobs and cries and starts that long journey into his own grief.

This movie is so powerful because it shows that by running from the lessons that we are presented only makes later lessons harder. It is as if Life is *determined* to get this man to feel, no matter what it takes. And it takes the near death of his son to finally get the man to wake up and begin to feel.

Now I want you to understand that Life does not act this way because it is mean, but because it knows that holding onto pain only causes deeper and more lasting pain. As you allow Life to show you your next step and you take, graciously, with all of the attendant feelings, you will find that your life will become richer and sweeter.

Another lesson that we cannot run from is whether we are teachers or not. *A Course in Miracles* tells us that we are teaching every moment of the day, whether we are aware of it or not. We are teaching either love or fear. We do not have a choice in whether we will teach. The only choice we have is *what* we will teach.

And what you teach determines what you think you are. If you teach hatred, you believe that you are hateful. If you lie, you believe you are a liar and you will distrust others. If you teach "an eye for an eye," you will also believe that you cannot be forgiven whenever you make a mistake.

If, on the other hand, you practice forgiveness, you will believe that you can also be forgiven. If you are willing to see the Christ nature in others, you will also be more able to see the Christ nature in yourself. We teach by example.

Now I never wanted to be a good example. When I was growing up, my mother would say to me,

"Be a good example to your brother."

The last thing I ever wanted to be was a good example to my brother. I was too busy growing up – just trying to be a boy. I was an avid reader but was supremely bored in school and so I was always getting into some kind of trouble. I was frequently caught in school reading from the wrong book, usually science-fiction. My mother was told that I would turn into a juvenile delinquent and she worried and fretted. She yelled at me. She pleaded with me. But to no avail.

During this period, one of my favorite statements to my mom was,

"I wanna do, what I wanna do!"

And I would do what I wanted to do. No matter what people said or did. And all the while my mom would ask,

"What kind of example are you to your brother?"

Well, the truth was – I didn't care!

Now even though I didn't want to be a good example, I did take mother's advice to always follow my own heart. I loved my little sisters and liked taking care of them and taking them to the library, even though my brother and my peers would make fun of me. I liked reading and peering into my microscope. My brother thought I was a dork.

But I secretly admired my brother. He was more out there. He was more glamorous. He was always getting into some kind of trouble. He was tough. He had hot girlfriends, ran with a wild crowd and had lots of adventures.

But even though I admired and envied him, that stuff just didn't appeal to me, and so I did what I wanted to do. I had my friends, swim team, reading, science, chess and girls.

And so, like brothers everywhere, we fought, taunted, hated and loved each other. And then we grew up and went our separate ways. We both went through marriages, divorces, new jobs and relationships. We even lived together in Seattle for a few months.

The night before I moved from Seattle to Houston, Jim and I had a goodbye supper together. Over a couple of beers, he told me,

"You know, Jer, when we were growing up, I always admired you."

"You did? Why?"

"Because you always did what you wanted to do. You didn't run with the crowd. You had a mind of your own. You didn't care what other people thought. I actually learned that from you."

And I thought to myself,

"What do you know! I was a good example after all!"

Even in the midst of disobedience and obstinacy, I was still teaching and my brother was still looking up to me, whether I wanted him to or not.

And now, I am a teacher and I teach others how to be good examples. Not how to be good little boys and girls, but how to be real and true to yourself, right or wrong. Live your life from the highest integrity you have. You don't have to be perfect, but be real. People, siblings, coworkers, the world is watching and learning from you, as you also learn from them.

And you will find that you cannot hide from love. It *will* find you, thank God!

Self Discovery Quiz

- *What are you teaching the world with your life?*

- *If there was a lesson you wanted the world to get, what would it be?*

- *Do you think that being a good example is a curse or a blessing? Why?*

- *Is it possible to be a good example without having to feel responsible all the time?*

- *What are your judgments of people who are good examples?*

- *What are your secret jealousies of people who are bad examples?*

- *Who in your life was a positive role model? What did they teach you? How old were you at the time?*

- *Do you think that people who are bad examples are somehow skipping growing up? Do you think that they are skipping their lessons? Is it possible for anybody to skip the lessons they need to learn?*

*Some people would be dead
if they only had the good sense
to stiffen.*

Joseph Heaney

*Breathing does not determine whether
a person is alive or not.
It just tells us which body
is ready for burial.*

Marlo Morgan – *Mutant Message*

*"Be a teacher, Richard. You'd be a good one.
An excellent one perhaps."
"But who would know?"
"You would know. Your students would
know. God would know. Not a bad public
at that!"*

Sir Thomas More to an ambitious court climber from
A Man for All Seasons

*I postpone death by living, by suffering, by
error, by risking, by giving, by losing.*

Anais Nin

Surviving a Near-Life Experience

So many times we hear about somebody who has a near death experience. And we get so caught up in the drama of the death and the visions that people see that we forget to look at what really is going on. The real lesson that I feel people learn from these experiences is that life is so precious and is always offering us unlimited opportunities to grow and learn.

In his book, *Return from Tomorrow,* George Richie experienced his near death. And what he says he regretted most as he reviewed all aspects and thoughts from his life, was that he didn't give and receive more love. Plain and simple. Not that he hadn't become a brilliant brain surgeon or a famous artist, but that love wasn't more of a part of his life.

So what are near life experiences? They are those times when we come closest to being fully open and alive. It's those moments when we are exposed to the possibility of love, support and new perceptions. It is being in the branch on the road and deciding for love instead of fear, acceptance rather than judgement, vision instead of blindness.

A Course in Miracles states that what we are really afraid of is love, not fear. I'm not talking about BIG love here, but everyday, common, garden-variety love. The bits of love, that added together, give us a full life. Some examples of a near life experience are:

- Taking time to listen to a mockingbird before going to work.

- Watching a bee gathering nectar.

- Watching the lightning in a storm.

- Listening to the rain.

- Receiving a compliment.

- Telling your children you love them and you are proud of them.

- Complimenting your lover.
- Waking early to see the sun rise.
- Letting somebody love you.
- Buying yourself a card or a flower even if you feel you don't deserve one.
- Just being you.

We get so busy *doing* life that we forget to just *be* and let life in. We are so busy trying to ford every stream and to climb the highest mountain that we forget that the true gift we are to this world is just being us, imperfect or not.

I remember once struggling with writing an article when a depressing feeling suddenly hit me. I felt that I would *probably* never write the Great-All-American-Novel, that I would never play piano in Carnegie Hall and that my art would never hang in any museum. Maybe it was Mid-life crisis, the blahs, judging myself too hard – whatever. I felt mediocre, the norm – just average – like everybody else.

I had always felt my destiny was to be someone special, to save the world – help people, open new doors. What I felt at that moment, though, was that not only was I going through the same doors that thousands had before – but I was banging my head on most of them.

The more I looked at the article I was trying to write, the dumber it looked. One moment it would look too cute, so I would tighten it up. Then it looked too serious, so I loosened it up. Now it looked flippant again. I just couldn't win! It was one of those days.

I threw the article on the desk in disgust and stormed out of the house for a long walk – to escape my mediocrity. It didn't help. My mediocrity followed me out.

When I got home I called my friend Lura for some support. I told her how my life felt so pointless, so ordinary, so meaningless. Where was my meaning in life?

"You mean you're not special?" she asked.

"No, I'm not. I feel like I'm supposed to do something great with my life. I'm supposed to make a difference in this world. But nothing's happening. I'm just stuck."

"You're just ordinary, aren't you."

"Yeah, and I'm tired of it! Nothing I do is great. I paint mediocre paintings, write mediocre stories, teach mediocre classes and play mediocre music. Where is my purpose?" I ranted.

"So, how does it feel to be ordinary?"

"Like everything else in my life – rotten"

"What would you say if I told you that there are lots of ordinary people out there who just want to hear an ordinary message?"

That stopped my whimpering long enough to make me think. My self pity dampened as she continued.

"Do you know that there are millions of people out there who don't feel like supermen? Who are afraid, like you, and would like to see an ordinary man doing ordinary things, telling an ordinary message in an ordinary way? There are people out there who judge themselves for not being supermen, when all the world needs is everyday, ordinary love."

Within minutes, she had me smiling and laughing at my situation.

That conversation got me excited again – about doing just an everyday job, but with love. Later I remembered an English comedy skit I once saw on TV. In it, everybody was a superman – housewives, business men, paper boys. Everybody wore a superman suit on with a big red "S" on the chest. And they could do super things – leap buildings, fly, haul boulders. They could do anything – except . . .

One day a little superboy's bicycle breaks down and he's sitting on the road, crying. Downtown, sensing that someone is in trouble, a businessman sneaks into a phone booth, changes, and comes out as – BICYCLE REPAIR MAN! He's wearing regular work clothes and he's carrying a toolbox. He runs to the boy, comforts him, fixes the bike and sends the boy on his way. He then returns to his everyday life. And all the other supermen and superwomen wonder who that repairman really was.

We spend our lives doing many superhuman feats. We handle stress, earn a living, raise children, pay the bills, have fights, make up. We leap stacks of paper in a single bound. We cook, eat, work and play faster than a speeding bullet. We get so busy being super that we forget to be us.

And in every one of us there is a Bicycle Repair Man. If we are attentive, we can let him/her out. Your child comes home from school crying and you stop for a moment and suddenly become "MOM." Or your son just wants time to play catch and you become "DAD." Or you lose your job and you become "VULNERABLE." Or your wife has a bad day and you become "HUSBAND." Or you look into each others eyes, time stops for a moment and you become "LOVERS." We stop and become ordinary, loving people.

A teacher once told me that masters are not people who do extraordinary things. Masters are people who do ordinary things in an extraordinary way. We all have unique gifts to offer this world. For some it will look like finding a cure for cancer or stopping war. For most, though, it will look like baking chocolate chip cookies, finalizing a good report, telling someone that you love them, or praising your child. Just the act of extending and receiving love is the best gift you can offer this world.

Make giving and receiving love a daily practice. Don't be afraid to make eye contact with the grocery clerk and to smile. When your child makes a mistake, instead of getting upset, don't be afraid to empathize on how rotten he may be feeling and give him reassurance and love. Even though you were first in line, don't be afraid to let a hurried person ahead of you. Don't resist going into your own backyard and enjoy nature. And thank the roses for their beauty and the dandelions for their tenacity. There is love for the taking and giving all around you!

Don't be afraid to open up and have a near-life experience.

Affirmations

- *God is always loving me and I am open to letting the love in.*

- *I love and appreciate my being ordinary.*

- *I can handle more love than I think I deserve.*

- *I am open to the unlimited possibilities that life is presenting to me right now!*

- *I now release and forgive myself for any missed opportunities. I am now ready for my next chance.*

- *Life always gives me millions of chances to let love in.*

- *I am open to letting the people in my life love me.*

- *I am open to loving all the people in my life.*

- *I no longer let any opportunity to love myself pass me by.*

- *I now face my fear of being loved completely and allow myself to experience all the feelings that come with it.*

- *I no longer judge my thoughts and feelings. I am safe.*

- *I now release my fear of being truly myself.*

*It is well to remember that a misplaced "I"
can transform the marital relationship
to a martial one.*

Anonymous

*If you have something to do
that is worthwhile doing,
don't talk about it,
but do it.
After you have done it,
your friends and enemies
will talk about it.*

George W. Blount

*Why not go out on a limb?
Isn't that where the fruit is?*

Frank Scully

*When you are good to others
you are best to yourself.*

Dr. Louis L. Mann

What's In It For Me?

In the movie *Field of Dreams*, there is a scene at the end that reveals a basic human truth about us. Shoeless Joe has just invited Terrance Mann to go out into the cornfield — the place where the spirits have been returning after every ballgame. And Ray gets mad.

"Why does *he* get to go?" he says. "Why not me?"

"Because you're not invited," replies Shoeless Joe.

"Not invited! Hey! I built this field! You guys are guests in my corn! I did everything that I was asked to do and not ONCE did I ask *'what's in it for me!'*"

"So what're you saying, Ray?"

"Well . . . . what's in it for me?"

Isn't that the truth sometimes? After all is said and done, after we've done X, Y and Z, ultimately what we want to know is "what's in it for me?". Even a totally generous act has a payoff — the feeling of doing good, the feeling that you are making the world a little better. But many of us feel that if we show any type of *selfish*, self centered thought, it somehow demeans the act, demeans us. It makes us less altruistic, less spiritual. Right?

Not so. We need to tell ourselves and others what it is we would like to receive out of any situation. When you have unexpressed desires and don't communicate them, what you create is a "hidden agenda." What this means is that though you may be doing whatever we agreed to, there is another secret goal that you are striving for. And it is possible for this secret goal to interfere with the whole purpose of why we are together in the first place.

What I want to stress here is that there is absolutely **nothing wrong** with having your own desires in any situation, but please, express them. Many of us have had the experience of giving and giving and never receiving anything in return. We then begin to think that we need to somehow trick the world into giving us what we want. We need to tell ourselves the *emotional* truth, that there are times when we feel like an empty pitcher, with nothing left to give — and the world just wants more and more. At times like that we just feel downright *resentful*.

This is the time to fill our pitcher.

The truth about us is that we are extensions of God's love and our *natural* tendency is to extend outward, to share our goodness, to share our love. But when we feel that there is nothing left to give, when we feel empty, we feel resentful. We don't like to admit these feelings, so we tend to cover it up with a spiritual, altruistic view. A man in my *Course in Miracles* class once said,

"All I ask for is for a woman to receive my love. I just want to give and have it received. No strings attached. She doesn't even have to reciprocate."

"Really?" I said. "That's great! I acknowledge you for being that giving. So you don't want anything from her?"

"No. She just has to receive my love."

"So if I'm hearing this right, it would be all right with you to be in a relationship with a woman, to love her, to give her compliments, to give her affection and gifts and it would be OK if she took your gifts and never responded. She acted like a stone. She ignored you."

"Well, no. I'd like *some* response. I'd want some affection back. I'd want . . ." He suddenly stopped and his eyes lit up. "Oh!" he exclaimed.

He realized at that moment that he did have expectations, wants and needs. He wanted to be loved in return — a very natural, human desire. What he needed to see was that it wasn't bad, materialistic or unspiritual to want it. The problems only arise when we **expect** it in return.

When somebody wants to volunteer, for example, in ushering at church, I ask them,

"What would you like to receive from this experience?"

This helps them to see that there is a benefit *for them* in volunteering. Too many people have the belief that it's expected of them to be volunteers, and what that creates are merely resentful helpers. People then begin to feel as if they're always giving with nothing in return. But when they acknowledge what they can receive, it gives a whole new slant.

"Maybe I'll meet some nice people."

"It would be fun collecting all that money from one row, pass it down the next and receive even more money on the next row. I love the thought of affirming that I am a channel and that money flows through me easily."

"I get the best parking space when I'm here early."

"Maybe I'll meet my future relationship."

No matter what the reason, though, give yourself permission to say,

"What's in it for me?"

Then you can give your love from a place of real love, caring, and passion. As *A Course in Miracles* relates,

The cost of giving is receiving.

Text pg. 255 / 275

and

Giving and receiving are the same.

Workbook Lesson #225

When you come from a place of true love, you will realize that you cannot give anything away without receiving. You will realize that when you give love, you receive the same in return. What's in it for you? The whole world.

Affirmations

- *I now forgive myself for the times I gave with strings attached.*

- *It is perfectly all right for me to receive whenever I give.*

- *As I become more honest with myself, the world becomes more honest with me.*

- *The world loves to hear what I want because the world loves to give to me.*

- *I now ask for what I want openly, honestly and lovingly.*

- *I love being rewarded for my efforts.*

- *God in me always guides my words when I am communicating my desires.*

- *Since the cost of giving is receiving, I am now willing to receive as I give.*

- *I have no resistance asking a fair price for my services.*

The greatest pleasure in life
is doing what people
say you cannot do.

Walter Bagehot

A child becomes an adult when he realizes
that he has a right not only to be right
but also to be wrong.

Thomas Szasz

When two men in business always agree,
one of them is unnecessary.

William Wrigley, Jr.

There are as many ways to live and grow
as there are people.
Our own ways are the only ways
that should matter to us.

Evelyn Mandel

The Right to Be Right

D o you ever remember a time, when you were having a fight with your relationship and you began to realize that maybe you didn't have all the facts, maybe you were wrong, but you still wanted to stick to your guns because. . . well, you just felt like a brat? You wanted to be right, no matter what. Or maybe there was a time when you were hurt by your relationship and your mate apologized but you just wanted to hang onto the hurt a little longer?

Well, it's OK to want to be right, even when you're wrong. It's OK to hang onto your hurt, your anger, your sadness as long as you don't blame the world for it. It's what I call being responsibly irresponsible. This is a place where even when the person we are fighting with apologized to us, we would still feel hurt. It takes time to release the hurt, and how long we want to hold onto it is our choice.

A Course in Miracles asks,

Do you prefer to be right or happy?

Text pg. 573/ 617

For me, many times, I preferred to be right. I preferred to view myself as a victim, as being picked on, as being misunderstood because actually, I *liked* the feeling. But once I gave myself permission to feel bad, to feel like a victim — right down to the soles of my feet — to blame the world for all my problems, after a while it got boring. There was a part of me that would just say,

"Do you *really* believe that all these people have been put on this world to *personally* torment you? C'mon, Jerry, let's get on with life!"

We have to **allow** ourselves to be right where we are in the moment. Too many times I'd given in before I was *emotionally* ready to surrender. And what happened was that later on, the unreleased anger would return and I would find myself snipping at my wife and making snide comments. Even though the argument was "over," I was still mad at her, and that unexpressed emotion demanded to be addressed. Usually she would pick up on it and pretty soon we were arguing all over again, but this time about something else.

 127

One time my wife and I were having a really big argument. We were yelling and screaming at each other, neither of us budging from our positions. I was damned if I was going to give in to her! We kept trying to convince the other that they were wrong. After about the fourth time of repeating the same issues, I yelled at her,

"Right now, I don't care about your side. I don't even care how you feel. I'm furious! I'm hurt. And I'm *not* going to budge."

She stopped arguing.

"In other words, Jerry, you just want to be right."

"Yeah. In fact, right now, I don't care if Jesus Christ Himself came down from Heaven to tell me I was wrong. I'd tell **Him** where to go!"

"So there's no way right now that I can win with you. There's no way that you'll listen to me, right now."

"Yep." I began to see how invested I was in my view. She smiled.

"So how long do you want to stay right?"

I couldn't stay totally angry at that point, because I was beginning to see how right I wanted to be. But I **was** still hurt and angry.

"I don't know. Give me an hour," I pouted.

"OK. I'll go in the other room and love myself, the best way I know how, and when you're ready, we can talk again."

It only took me about twenty minutes of sulking before I got tired of being "right" about women and I went to her and we talked this time. I listened to her side, being willing to be wrong and happy and then she listened to my side, also being willing to be wrong and happy. We began to share what was really going on, our hurts and fears. We shared who our partner was reminding us of from our past. And soon, we were both happy. We both shifted our views.

We have found this to be a very powerful tool when having an argument. Just to acknowledge those times when we are more interested in being right, that we **are** invested in our hurt, gives the other person an opportunity to back off and stop beating their heads against our wall. We all need time to feel the hurt, feel our victim thoughts and then let them go. *But let the world (your relationship, especially) know that you need this time.* What I have found is that sooner or later, the pain of being separate, the pain of hating my wife hurts more than hanging onto the issue. Then it becomes more important to return to the love and I am willing to hear her side.

It's OK to want to be right. It's OK to be stuck. Just let the other person know. And then choose whether you want to be right — or happy.

Affirmations

- *I now give myself permission to feel and express all my true feelings.*

- *I no longer judge myself for being human.*

- *I am now willing to be happy, no matter what the outcome may be.*

- *I am God with skin on.*

- *People love when I express my truth.*

- *It is safe to nurture and love the little child within.*

- *I now forgive myself for the times I expressed my feelings inappropriately.*

- *God is always speaking through me.*

If you stop every time a dog barks,
your road will never end.

Arabian proverb

Even if you're on the right track,
you'll get run over if you just sit there.

Will Rogers

A ship in harbor is safe,
but that is not what ships are built for.

John A. Shedd, *Salt from My Attic*

Triumph is just "umph" added to "try."

Anonymous

Anything Worth Doing
by Jerry Stefaniak

"Anything worth doing, is worth doing well"
That's a cute little phrase that has kept me in hell

Why should I try, or practice at all?
I'll not play the Met or Carnegie Hall.

My drawings are silly, they don't make people move
They'll never be famous, or hang in the Louvre.

Trying new things is a risk we all take
But you might botch it up, you can't make a mistake.

So I just gave up, many things were not tried
I suppressed my adventure, and part of me died.

Then one day, I raised up my fist
For the chances I'd lost and the joys that I'd missed.

I was tired of watching my life pass me by
I didn't want to grow old and say "Why didn't I try?"

Then I had a new thought, a thought to be free
"I can do what I want, I can do it for me!"

And I started my music, my writing, my art
I let go of perfection, I just came from my heart.

Canvas was ruined, flat notes were played
Stories were written, with plots that would fade.

But through all my efforts I shattered the Hell
"Stop looking to others — in **your** way, excel"

I like what I do, I am pleased by my craft
To those old, hurtful thoughts, I have simply laughed

Don't rationalize ever, anything that you do
Forget what they say, just do it for you.

There are joys to experience, like the stars, they are myriad
Anything worth doing — is worth doing . . . period.

Finding Heaven

A man who had lost his house keys was looking for them near a street lamp. A friend joined him and together they proceeded to look. After quite a while of fruitless searching, the friend finally asked,

"Mustapha, are you sure you dropped your keys here?"

"Oh no," replied Mustapha, "I lost them somewhere in the alley."

"Well, why aren't we looking there?"

"Because the light's better here."

We have spent thousands of years looking for that ultimate utopia, our paradise, the final peace. But we have been looking in the wrong place. It's been easier to blame someone else than to go into our hearts and look inside. Jesus said *"The kingdom of Heaven is, Lo, not here nor there, but the Kingdom of Heaven is within."*

Blessed is he who expects nothing,
for he shall never be disappointed.

Jonathan Swift

God gives every bird its food,
but He does not
throw it into the nest.

J. G. Holland

Cats seem to go on the principle
that it never does any harm
to ask for what you want.

Joseph Wood Krutch

Dear God — I pray for patience.
And I want it right now!

Oren Arnold

Just Ask

The first step in getting the things you desire is to first get clear on what it is you want and then — ask for it.

For many of us, by the time we were ten, we had heard the word "No!" so many times, that ultimately we assumed that that was the answer we would always hear. And so we stopped asking, and worse yet, we stopped dreaming.

Oh, we may be aware of the obvious things, like money or relationships, but there are *little* things that are really important, that we just let die. One of the first questions I ask of a new client is,

"What do you want to receive out of these sessions? What do you want out of life?"

Most of them go blank. They've suppressed their wishes for so long, that they cannot even express them. Luckily, with a little work, the asking muscle can be reawakened and it's wonderful to see a person begin to ask and dream once again. Why is it important to ask for what you want? Because not only do we inform God and the world what it is we desire, but, it also lets us in on the secret. The speaker Mark Victor Hansen has people list 101 goals or things that they want to achieve. The miracle of doing something like this is that over time, many of those written goals are attained. Once the mind has been programmed to receive these goals, we naturally gravitate toward them.

When we were growing up, we had to live by somebody else's rules and then, we carried those rules into our adulthood. Rules like:

"There's never enough, so don't even ask."

"You have to sacrifice for the good of all."

"If I give this to you, there won't be anything for your sister," and on and on . . .

Well, I have a new rule for you:

You are now an adult and the rules have changed! You are now the Maker of rules!

For starters ask yourself,

"What are the odds of getting all or even part of what I want, if I ask for it?"

50%? 30%? Even 10%?

Now ask,

"What are my odds of getting what I want if I **don't** ask?"

A big, fat zero. If nobody knows what you want (especially you), you'll never get it.

A company that I once worked for used to subsidize the cafeteria so it was possible to get a decent lunch for about $1.50. One day they were serving pork chops. Now, I *love* pork chops. But all you got was one. I wanted another so I asked if I could buy a second one. To my surprise, the server said, "Of course" and I paid just a little more. When I got to my table, my buddies looked at my plate,

"Hey, how do you rate two pork chops? You got a girlfriend behind the counter?"

I laughed and said that I just asked for another and paid extra.

"I didn't know we could do that," said a friend.

Well, neither did I — until I asked. Since that time, I have learned to ask for everything I want. From relationships, from parents, from bosses, from teachers, from myself and, most important of all, from God. And I have been surprised at how giving and open the world has become.

Another objection I hear, most often in relationships, is,

"If I have to ask him for what I want, I don't want it!"

So many people deprive themselves of the joy of life because they are so resentful of past hurts, and will not *demean* themselves into asking for what it is they want. It's crazy. They expect the world *to know* what it is they want and to give it to them, without their having to ask. And yet, I have never heard anybody say,

"If **I** have to ask God for what I want, I don't want it!"

They pray and pray and when they receive, they thank God. They don't expect God to read their minds (even though He can), but they expect others to read their minds (even though they can't).

Another saying we hear so often is,

"If you loved me, you would know what I want."

This comment neglects one important fact. It omits the fact that we are human, that we forget to think of others at times. Yes, I know my wife likes cards and flowers and hugs and kisses, but there are times, many times, that I forget. I get tied up in **my** world and get so full of myself, I forget that there are other people. What my wife has discovered is that I like to give her hugs and kisses and flowers, but sometimes I need to be reminded.

And so, she asks. For a hug, a kiss, a compliment or reassurance. And she receives it. I have also learned to ask her for the same things. It is a wonderful feeling to ask for reassurance or a hug, especially on those days when you feel most unlovable, and then to receive it. It feels great to realize that we are the masters of our universe. That we decide what it is we want and whether we get it or not.

What happens if you ask and do not receive? Well, we can still grow from the experience. Remember the chapter about the world always reflecting our innermost thoughts? If you are asking and not receiving what you are asking for, ask yourself why you don't want to receive it. Ask yourself, "What suppressed thoughts are blocking my abundance? In what ways do I feel that I don't deserve more money, a better relationship or forgiveness?"

Or write yourself a letter stating why you are not ready to receive what you are asking for. If you have a hard time doing this, then *just pretend* that you **really** do not want what you are asking for. You'll be surprised at what will show up. You will begin to realize that there are conflicting thoughts around anything you desire. Once you become aware of the thoughts that are keeping you stuck, then you can develop affirmations to plant new thoughts. You can seek out reading material that teaches a greater prosperity consciousness. You can ask friends, a minister or a counselor for help. Either way, whether you receive what you ask for or not, you can learn.

Finally, an unexpected payoff that we receive when we ask is in the area of forgiveness. Whenever you ask somebody for what you want, what you are doing, on another level, is actually forgiving somebody from your past who once said "no." You are in effect affirming that that person did not squash your desires or your dreams. Truly, you are acting *as if* they never hurt you.

What you are implicitly saying is,

"See, dad, you didn't stop my aliveness by saying 'no.' I still ask and I still dream. You didn't hurt me."

Do you want to open up your life to more joy, love and excitement?

Well, start asking

Self Discovery Quiz

- *Name three things that you would like your relationship to do for you.*

- *What was the most outrageous request you ever had concerning sex?*

- *When is the last time you asked for a hug?*

- *If God gave you a signed, blank check, how much would you make it out for?*

- *When is the last time you asked your boss for anything?*

- *What do you want more of in your job? List five items.*

- *What do you want more of in your relationship? List five items.*

- *What do you want more of from your children? List five items.*

- *What do you want more of from God? List five items.*

- *When is the last time you treated yourself to a hot fudge sundae, a piece of pie with ice cream or your favorite candy?*

*Those who bring sunshine
to the lives of others
cannot keep it from themselves.*

Anonymous

*When we do the best that we can,
we never know what miracle is wrought
in our life, or in the life of another.*

Helen Keller

*It is the greatest of all mistakes to do
nothing because you can do only a little.
Do what you can.*

Sydney Smith

*A teacher affects eternity;
he can never tell where
his influence stops.*

Henry Adams, *The Education of Henry Adams*

You Make a Difference

The thing that kept me from writing this book earlier is that I got stuck in one of the oldest ego traps in the world — the thought that I don't make a difference. When we look at the world through the ego's eyes, it does seem as if we are a mere speck of dust in the universe, only one voice in a mass of billions, and our egos want us to believe that. The last thing they want us to see is that we possibly can change our world and that it is in our hands.

But there are numerous examples of one person making a difference. Mahatma Gandhi is my favorite example. This was a man who stood by his dream to free India and through his demonstration and commitment, rallied a whole nation behind him. And after India was free and the people began fighting among themselves, he alone was able to stop the bloodshed through peaceful means. He was a man who inspired millions of people all over the world.

Martin Luther King was a man who stood against the racial prejudice of the times, to tell his message and make a difference. But I don't want to dwell on the famous figures of the past. It becomes too easy for our egos to say,

"Well that was just them. They were already famous and had people behind them."

So we won't talk about when they were "nobodies", scared and doubtful, like the rest of us. Or when they became famous but were **still** scared and doubtful, like the rest of us. What I want to concentrate here is on how we all make a difference in this world, whether we realize it or not. *A Course in Miracles* states that all expressions of love are maximal. That there is no difference between a "small" act of love and a "large" act of love. What matters is that love is expressed in the first place. It is our own egos that judge the effectiveness of our gestures.

How do we make a difference? By being the best person we know how, in the moment, by baking chocolate chip cookies with love, by listening to our lover, by balancing that report at work with care, by living life with excitement and enthusiasm. By forgiving others for their misdeeds and forgiving ourselves for our own. By giving that all important hug to our children, when their world is falling down. By giving ourselves a hug when ours is crumbling too.

We touch people in ways we never expected. A gentle smile, a loving caress, a kind word can be the catalyst that alters a person's day, or even their life. Have you ever had an instance when you were feeling down and unlovable and somebody, a waitress, for example, just said,

"Don't worry about it, honey, it'll get better. Here, have some more coffee" — and changed your mood? Didn't it feel good? The movie *It's a Wonderful Life* is an example of how important we are to the world. What a big hole we would leave behind if we never existed! Like pieces of a puzzle, every person adds their part to our lives. Some make it better, some harder. But we don't know until we stand back and see the whole spectrum of our life, with all the colors and shapes, that we realize what a gift our lives can be.

Eric Butterworth tells a story about a man who made a difference in somebody's life and was lucky enough to find out. One morning, as a man was rushing to his train, he dropped a few dollars in a beggar's cup as he passed by. Suddenly the man stopped, returned to the beggar and said,

"I almost forgot. You're a businessman, too", and took some of his pencils. He then went on his way to work.

Months later, at an evening conference, the same businessman was approached by a man in an old, but neatly pressed suit.

"You probably don't know who I am, but three months ago I was begging in the streets. I had no job, no self esteem, no money. You came by one day, gave me money and took my pencils and you reminded me that I was a businessman too. That one remark stuck with me and I began to *feel* like a businessman. I began to *act* like a businessman and I began to *see* myself as a businessman. I was not a beggar. I was a businessman. As you can see, I am no longer a beggar. I am a businessman. Thanks."

How many times have we changed somebody's life, just like that, and never found out?

We all make a difference. The Universe is just waiting for us to realize the part we play. Two quotes from *A Course in Miracles* address this.

God Himself is incomplete without me.

Text 165/177

and

You are altogether irreplaceable in the Mind of God. No one else can fill your part in it, and while you leave your part of it empty your eternal place merely waits for your return.

Text 166/179

Remember, it's not whether we find the cure to cancer or stop all of the hunger in the world. What matters is when we brighten a person's shattered world with a smile, a touch or even a chocolate chip cookie. What matters is when we appease the hunger for love in one person's heart. The light from a candle — no matter how small — illuminates areas we are not even aware of. The light of our love expands and shines on other people, affecting them in ways we cannot imagine. It warms and it illuminates. Let your love expand, because *you do make a difference*. The world needs your gift. So start taking action!

Self Discovery Quiz

- *How do you make a difference to —*
  your relationship?
  your children?
  your boss?
  your co-workers?
  the waitress that serves you coffee?

- *What would your world look like if you never existed? Whose life would be affected?*

- *What is a small expression of love that gives you a lot of pleasure when you perform it? When is the last time you did it?*

- *What have you always secretly wanted to be when you grow up? What's stopping you?*

- *What was the nicest thing a teacher ever did for you?*

- *What was the nicest thing a co-worker ever did for you?*

- *What was the nicest thing a boss ever did for you?*

- *What was the nicest thing a parent ever did for you?*

- *Have you ever done a kind act without anybody ever finding out?*

- *When is the last time you complimented your lover, child or co-worker?*

Appreciation of what we have
is at least one-half
of the true way of life.

Anonymous

Some may have more material goods
than others
but no man is poor
who has eyes to see,
ears to hear, and,
above and beyond all,
a heart to understand.

Alma Weizelbaum, *Wealth*

Bitterness imprisons life;
love releases it.

Harry Emerson Fosdick

It must be aggravating to be an atheist
and create a miracle
and then have nobody to thank.

Anonymous

Thank You, God, and Send Me More

Do you want a little method that will enhance your prosperity and help you to realize what a wonderful life you have? Start thanking God and the people in your life. Start thanking God for what you have and the abundance that is coming your way.

Gratitude is the quickest way to change your attitude about life. When you are grateful for the things you currently have, you begin to appreciate what you already created. When you are grateful for what you already have, the universe begins to supply more. Remember that the world "out there" is a reflection of our own minds. When we complain and grumble about life we change from "Christians" into "Mr. Christian" and create our own Mutiny with Our Bounty. When we complain, there is no room for the Holy Spirit to work. We are so busy being right about how bad life is, we miss the flowers that are along the path. In fact, we trample them.

Years ago, my teacher, Joe Heaney, had all of us students do a little exercise that turned my thoughts around about money. We were all resentful and grumbling at the time about our financial situations. We were pissed at him for having to pay for our classes, we were pissed at the city for the electric bills, we were pissed at our creditors for always hounding us. In short, we were pissed at everybody and there wasn't a lot of room for God to work.

One day, Joe had all of us bring our checkbooks to class. He asked me to open to any page and read off who the first check was made out to.

"Visa, for $50."

"And who received the benefits?"

"Visa did."

"No, Jerry, who received the benefits of the services?"

"What do you mean?"

"What did you charge?"

"A couple of dinners, a trip to Hawaii, some clothes."

"So, who received the benefits of having that card?"

It took me a minute to understand where he was going.

"**I** received the benefits."

"Good, what's the next check?"

"GMAC — my car payment."

"Who received the benefits of the car?"

"I did"

"The next check?"

"Seattle Power and Light."

"Who received the heating and lighting?"

"I did."

And on and on it went. I could not find one check that I didn't *personally* receive some benefit. Every check was written for me! I just didn't want to take responsibility for them. I was so busy blaming the credit card companies, blaming the government, blaming the car industry, that I couldn't even receive the gifts that were already mine! I had paid for them but I never totally received them.

After that I began to write "Thank You" in the memo space of my checks. I still do. At first it wasn't easy. It was amazing how angry and resentful I felt toward the world. It wasn't surprising that my life was full of lack. That's all I acknowledged I had! But after a few checks, I began to smile and then to laugh. You see, as I wrote *thank you* on each check, my mind would automatically remind me of why I was thanking my creditor.

"Oh yeah, Jerry, remember that dinner at the Space Needle? It was nice. And it's nice to have heat and light. And your car does get you around."

What? You have nothing to be thankful for? Are you reading this book? Thank God for being able to see. Can you feel the pages? Thank God for your body. Are you sitting in a nice chair? Thank God for the chair. Are you comfortable? Thank God for your environment. Make thanking God a daily ritual. Thank Him for where you live, the hot shower you take, the breakfast you eat and the job you have. There were times in my life when all I felt I could thank God for was a warm shower and my health. But the more I thanked God and others, the more I began to draw to myself. I began to feel abundance, *regardless* of how my finances looked.

I want to be crystal clear here about having an attitude of gratitude. Feeling grateful is not just a nice little, New-Age exercise you can do. It is not a way to cover over your problems with a veneer of Pollyanna thoughts. Gratitude (along with forgiveness) is one of the most powerful ways of marshalling your love and energy. It actually changes your energetic vibration to a higher frequency. And your body then responds physically, shifting from adrenaline to endorphins. And from this higher vibration, your attitudes and perceptions about life change. And from there, your life *will* always change for the better. The Japanese have a saying,

"Appreciation is the highest vibration."

In her tape on *Spiritual Madness*, Carolyn Myss tells the story of a man who had a near death experience. As he floated above his body, an angel asked him whether he would like to see his life from a different perspective. Not knowing any better or what was in store, he said, "Yes. Of course."

And what was shown to him were all of the incidences of his life that were hard and troubled. But they were shown from the point of view of what *could have happened* if only he had shown a *little gratitude* and appreciation for what he already had. In every case, he got to see people (or angels) who wanted to help but his own self-indulgence and resentment kept them away.

You will never know how close love and help is until you are willing to open up to it – no matter what. And gratefulness *always* opens the heart.

I remember a time, right after I had moved to Houston. I was sitting in a grocery store parking lot with only $2.58 in my pocket and I remember feeling more prosperous then I had ever felt in my life. True, I had no money, but I was surrounded by friends, a new family and people whom I cared for. I felt rich.

I began to realize that God was always pouring the riches of Life onto me and I was the one wearing a raincoat! I was the one holding up an umbrella! I had the thought, that night, that I could not *conceive* of how much God wanted to give me. And so I created a little exercise to expand my receiving consciousness. Whenever I create receiving anything, whether it be a penny on the street, a compliment, or a raise, I look to God in my heart and say,

"Thank you, God, send me more."

What this affirms is that I received the gift and I am still open to receive *even more* from the Universe. So many people will ignore picking up a penny, thinking that a penny does not matter. But they don't realize that the penny represents the **part of their minds** that is giving them money. If you cannot receive a penny, then you cannot receive a dime, or a dollar, or a raise. Start affirming that you are ready to receive more and more from the universe. And start today.

Another powerful idea, from Susan Jeffer's book *Feel the Fear and Do It Anyway*, is to make a gratitude book. A gratitude book is simply a book that lists everything that you are grateful for. Every date you had, all the sex you enjoyed, every gift you received, every sunset. Listing every wonderful thing in your life slowly gets your mind into looking at only the good — at the joy you've already experienced. Right now, my gratitude book has around 500 items. And you know what? It doesn't matter how bad things are going, I cannot look into my gratitude book without smiling — even just a little. As I once again reap the harvest of those past joys, it lifts me up to realize how rich my life has been that these things will be experienced again.

When Jesus performed the miracle of feeding five thousand people with a few loaves and fishes, He didn't look down at the food and say,

"This will never feed all these people."

The first thing He did was to turn His eyes towards heaven and **give thanks to His Father.** He thanked God for what He already had and for what He was about to do. Jesus knew that God's universe is an abundant universe. Jesus knew that God is ever present and just waiting to work through us. Jesus **knew** that gratitude should be as natural as breathing. Not only was He able to feed five thousand people, but when all the leftovers were collected, there were thirteen baskets full of food remaining.

Do you want to feel better about your life? Do you want to feel what a gift you are to the world? Do you want to see the blessings that are already in your world? Then start by looking at what you already have and just say,

"Thank you, God! And send me more!"

Self Discovery Quiz

- *Do you have a hard time saying "thanks" for any kind deed?*

- *What is the last acknowledgment that you gave your relationship?*

- *What are three things you can thank your mother for?*

- *What are three things you can thank your father for?*

- *What are three things you can thank your boss for?*

- *What are three things you can thank yourself for?*

- *What are three things you can thank your relationship for?*

- *What are three things you can thank God for?*

If you begin by sacrificing yourself
to those you love,
you will end up hating those to whom
you have sacrificed yourself.
Self sacrifice is suicide.
George Bernard Shaw

The mother who gives up her life
for her children does them no kindness
but rather burdens them
with the legacy of a life unlived.
Janet Falldron

Sacrificers are not the ones to pity.
The ones to pity are those they sacrifice.
Elizabeth Bowen

Life is made up, not of great sacrifices and
duties, but of little things,
in which smiles and kindness,
and small obligations,
given habitually,
are what win and preserve
the heart and secure comfort.
Sir Humphrey Davy

Letting Go of Sacrifice

Do you want to continue feeling resentful towards life and the world? Do you want to feel angry all the time, unappreciated and used? Do you like feeling like a victim? Then sacrifice every chance you get, because nothing stirs up resentment and anger like good old fashioned sacrifice. Sacrifice is a cute little trick that the ego plays in order to make us pay for guilt and to keep ourselves and others in control. In ancient times we sacrificed food, animals, even people to appease the gods and help us to feel a little less guilty. We even have the thought that God sacrificed Jesus, in order to pay for our sins.

Before I get into the dynamics of sacrificing, I want to address the concept about Jesus "dying for our sins." *A Course in Miracles* takes on this issue quite frankly. In short, Jesus says that He did not die for our sins because we have **always been innocent.** What He was attempting to teach us was that our bodies are not real. That our True selves are eternal. That men could whip Him, beat Him, nail Him to a tree and three days later He would return. The crucifixion was meant to be an extreme learning device to illustrate this point. It was meant to show that we are more powerful than we ever dreamed. For three years beforehand, Jesus constantly said,

"All this and more will you do!"

I believe He wasn't kidding when He said that. He meant it literally. Heal the sick, feed the hungry and even conquer death personally. What Jesus was trying to teach in those three years was that we are creators and no different than Him. That we are much more powerful and wonderful than we realize. Whenever He healed somebody, He generally had two favorite sayings,

"Your sins are forgiven. Go in peace." Or,

"Your faith has saved you."

Remember, Jesus was talking the vernacular of the times. In those days, people believed that disease was caused by sins from the person, his parents, or other ancestors. What Jesus did was to reflect, however briefly, the Christ that was **already in the person.** For a moment, guilt was dropped, the person saw who they really were and were cured. Jesus never said that He cured the sick. He was the catalyst through which miracles happened, if the mind of the sick person was fertile. You may recall that there were towns where Jesus could not perform miracles. The people there simply were not open to new thought.

Jesus says in *A Course in Miracles* that sacrifice is a tool of the ego and that God does not ask for sacrifice from His Sons. Sacrifice is nothing but a vicious trap. Why?

Let me explain what's called the Wheel of Sacrifice. This concept was first explained to me by Rev. Phil Smedstad. When we sacrifice, what normally occurs is that we have unexpressed expectations. We do something with the thought that someday we'll be repaid. Of course, we don't let anybody know. For example,

"I'll raise you and then you'll take care of me when I'm old and gray."

"I'll do all these things for her, and maybe I'll get some sex."

So the wheel starts like this:

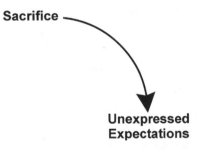

When we don't express what it is we expect (remember the chapter on asking for what you want?), and then get nothing in return, how do we feel? We feel disappointed:

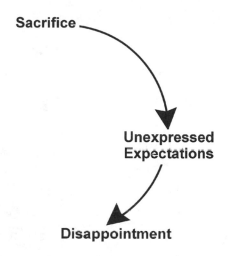

When we feel disappointed, what is the next feeling we usually feel? ANGER! And anger **always** gets expressed, in one way or another — and so we attack.

We blame the other person (*"After all I've done for you! After all I've sacrificed!"*) for not fulfilling their part of the bargain. Now, attack, no matter how "justified," never feels good. That brings up one of the ego's favorite feelings — guilt.

And when we feel guilty, what do we think we need to do to stop feeling the guilt? Sacrifice some more!

If you tell yourself the truth, you will realize that this is how the world operates. Sacrifice, unexpressed expectations, disappointment, anger, guilt, and then sacrifice again. Round and round it goes, with the guilt and resentment building with each cycle. The wheel will run forever, until somebody stops it.

Families are run by this concept, religions are run by this concept, businesses are run by this concept, even nations are run by this concept. And all of it is done unconsciously in an effort to not feel guilty.

Since all of this sacrificing is unconscious, how can we become aware of it in the first place? Well, have you ever had this experience? You do something for somebody in the highest, most altruistic motive, and then something happens, things don't turn out as you expected. Maybe that person doesn't even thank you! And you feel angry and resentful. That is unconscious sacrificing. Even though you *thought* you were coming from a place of unconditional love, there were still strings attached. You had a secret agenda.

Here are some other common symptoms of sacrifice:

- You feel resentful and angry and you don't even know why. Or maybe you just feel angry with others because they don't seem to appreciate you.

- You expect others to sacrifice for you.

- You keep hoping that someday, somebody will recognize all that you have done for them and then it will be your turn.

- You feel used and unappreciated.

- You keep giving and giving but it never seems to be enough.

- You feel sorry for yourself a lot, like a martyr.

- You feel guilty whenever you say "no".

- You are afraid to hurt other people's feelings and so you don't set boundaries and thereby hurt yourself.

- You find yourself coming from a place of "*I should*" instead of "*I choose to.*"

A Course in Miracles states that sacrifice is an attack on the other person. Sacrifice is an example of "giving" in order to "get". All the while that you are giving with one hand, the other hand is under the table, waiting for the payoff. Nobody ever wins or feels successful in a relationship like that. How many relationships are based on the concept of obligation and duty? How many relationships die because of unfulfilled obligations? Whenever you feel like somebody "owes" you for something, know that sacrifice has been operating.

How do you break the Wheel of Sacrifice? Well, first you must become aware that you are doing it and then start reversing the cycle.

But now comes the tricky part because as you stop sacrificing, you will have to go back through the Wheel of Sacrifice, only in reverse. And all of the feelings that you have been avoiding by sacrificing will have to be addressed. So let's go back down the wheel and see what happens.

When you stop sacrificing, the first feeling that hits you (like a locomotive) is guilt.

Bob Mandel, in his book *Open Heart Therapy*, describes guilt as the "mafia of the mind." It is like this brute who visits you periodically to get his weekly payoff. And if you do not pay up (sacrifice), he will sit on your chest until you do. Our egos know that nobody likes to feel guilty, so it thinks that if it can make you feel guilty long enough, you'll relent and start sacrificing again. This is the place where you have to allow yourself to feel the discomfort as you begin to say "no" and you stick to it.

If you have been sacrificing for some time, be prepared for the people in your life to try to guilt-trip you to get you back in line.

There is a story I once heard about a man who called his mother who was excellent in manipulating feelings.

"So, Mom, how are you doing?"

"Oh," she replied, "I'm feeling a little weak. I haven't eaten in over ten days."

"Ten days!" he exclaimed. "Why haven't you been eating?"

"Well, I didn't want to have my mouth full in case you called."

The important thing I want to stress here is that every negative feeling *has an end* to it. What I have learned is that if I allow myself to *feel* guilty but I do not *act* as if I was guilty, ultimately the feeling lessens and then leaves.

So then after we process our guilt (or even in conjunction), we are then accosted with our repressed anger.

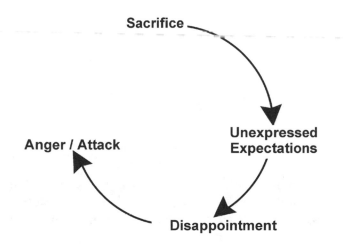

We will begin to feel anger at all the times we sacrificed. For all the times we didn't ask for what we wanted - that kiss, that hug, that acknowledgement. For not taking the chance to open up to more possibilities. We may also feel angry at all the people in our life who expect us to sacrifice for them. Also, once again, if you have trained the people in your life to expect you to sacrifice, they will get angry at you for changing the rules.

Now remember, the important thing here is to persevere past these feelings. There will come a time when these feelings will lessen and you will also learn how to live your life as you are feeling these feelings. The thing I want to stress here is that once you see the pain, hurt, guilt and anger that sacrifice breeds, you'll never want to go back.

Then we get to process our disappointments.

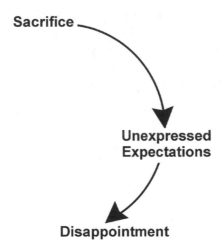

Sacrifice

Unexpressed Expectations

Disappointment

I heard of a title of a book that really speaks to me – *If You Want Guarantees, Get a Toaster*. There are no guarantees in life and we are very apt to be disappointed. The crazy thing is that sacrifice is a way of trying to guarantee that the other person will act the way we expect them to act. We are trying to control our disappointment. But when we stop trying to control others, we find that we actually have more time and energy for all the dreams that we have been putting on the back burner.

And finally we get to look at our unexpressed expectations.

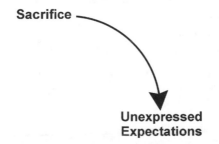

Sacrifice

Unexpressed Expectations

Initially you may feel ashamed and stupid as you uncover all of your hidden agendas. This is a time for you to really practice compassion for yourself – *no matter what*. Begin to dig down into your psyche and tell yourself the truth about what you expect out of life. Maybe you expect life to treat you fairly because you had a hard childhood. Maybe you unconsciously expect your partner to buy you everything because of poverty you endured. Maybe you expect God to come through and give to you because you've given up eating meat, or been celibate or just because you've suffered long enough.

But when you let go of trying to get other people to fulfill you, you then have to rely on the only person who can truly fulfill you – YOU! And believe me! That is a wonderful place to be.

Now this doesn't mean that you shouldn't have people in your life that help and assist you as you grow. But when two people come together with the purpose of giving and receiving love with no strings attached, that is true love.

So get off the Wheel! Begin to ask for what it is that you want. Tell your partner, lover or child what it is that you expect for doing something and let them agree or not agree to the terms. If you agree to do something for another, check in your heart and see if you are coming from a place of expecting something in return. Or see if you are depriving yourself of anything. Become conscious of your hidden desires and expectations.

When I initially suggest this to a family, instantly you can see the fear arise. Most people have this thought that if we stop sacrificing, the family (and the world) will break down — nothing will get done and there will be chaos. At first, there usually *is* chaos. But that is only normal as the family is learning a new set of rules.

For example, when mom stops cooking all the time because nobody appreciates her cooking, it looks for a while as if the whole family unit has gone to hell. But after a few weeks, a wonderful thing begins to happen.

You see, we *naturally* love our families. We naturally care for our children. After a period of time when people have an opportunity to fill their empty pitchers, the love begins to overflow. Mom begins to think it would be nice to bake her favorite lasagna casserole because — well, she misses doing it and she loves her family.

Now the parent is coming from a different tack. Now she is cooking and cleaning because she cares and it's one of the ways she expresses her love to her family.

And the children benefit. As they see their parents asking for what they want, as they see their parents' self esteem grow, they learn that it is OK to ask for what they want. That sacrifice is no longer how to relate to each other, but love is. And now the children no longer have to feel guilty because their parents sacrifice for them.

You see, I used to believe that unless somebody sacrificed, people would become selfish and not care about anybody else. That all of the *dirty* jobs that nobody likes to do would be left undone. That the garbage would never be collected and good streets would never be built or maintained. But over the years it has been my pleasure to meet people who have shown me something different. I had a student in one of my classes who became very wealthy as a garbage man. He was actually excited and inspired about running and maintaining a waste management company. And he was good at it and he did an excellent job. Another student of mine related a story how she heard about a man who was challenged and excited about creating new and improved road surfaces. He also became quite rich by building and repairing roads. These men were not sacrificing. But they saw a need and they knew that they had a gift in responding to that need. And, of course, the world rewarded them.

When you come from a place of *choice* rather than *obligation*, you no longer feel resentful. From there you give from a place of fullness and extension, you give with a full heart, with no strings attached. Do you want to build a better world order? Then it's time to sacrifice your sacrifice.

Self Discovery Quiz

- *What am I doing now that I resent?*

- *Am I doing anything now for my lover in which I secretly expect them to someday pay me back?*

- *Do I expect my children to take care of me when I am old?*

- *When somebody gives me a compliment, do I feel compelled to return the favor?*

- *Do I give with an open heart or are there conditions attached?*

- *Who gives more in my relationship? I or my partner?*

- *When someone sacrifices for me, do I feel the need to sacrifice for them? How can I stop it?*

- *Are you in a job because you fell somebody has to do it, and it might as well be you?*

*For peace of mind,
resign as general manager
of the universe.*

Larry Eisenberg

*Learn to bend.
It's better than breaking.*

Anonymous

*When a man takes one step toward God,
God takes more steps toward the man
than there are sands in the worlds of time —
this is called the welcoming of God,
or the Kaballah.*

The Work of the Chariot

In God We Trust.

Motto of the United States

Nuts!

During the Battle of the Bulge, General Anthony McAllife was presented a request to surrender from a messenger from the German army. His immediate reply was "Nuts!"

Funny thing. That is what most of my clients say when I inform them that in order to heal their relationships, or create more money in their lives, or create that perfect job, they will have to surrender their thoughts of how it should look. What is the first thought that comes to your mind when the word surrender is mentioned? A white flag? A doormat? A person with bootprints across their chest? Many people think that if they surrender, they will lose.

Surrender is not a four-letter word. Contrary to popular opinion, surrender is not an act of weakness, especially when it comes to relationships and self growth. The original, archaic definition of surrender was *"to release to another what was originally theirs in the first place."* When a baron surrendered land to the king, he was acknowledging that the land belonged to the king and he was his servant. So what is it in relationships that already belongs to another that we need to surrender? How about **respect, love** and **honesty**? Don't we all deserve that? Surrender allows. Surrender invites. Surrender gives a person the opportunity to see another side. Ultimately, surrender acknowledges that we are invulnerable, safe spirits, and that nothing is ever lost or stolen. When you surrender to a higher power or your relationship, you give that higher power (or relationship) a chance to work, a chance to show you their side.

Now some of you may be saying,

"Hey, earlier you said to ask for what you want but now you're saying to surrender. What gives?"

You should always ask for what you want because that concentrates the power of your mind, but in the same breath, also be willing to surrender to God what you receive and how you receive it. Be willing to know that you will always get what is best for all concerned. You see, most of the time we do not know our own best interests. For example, we may think our problem is not enough money and we have to receive it in a certain manner. But God may see a better solution to our problem — one not even connected with money. So when I pray to God for something I usually pray something like this:

"Dear God, if I can have it **my** way, help me to create that perfect job and more money in my life. And help me to remove any barriers I have to receiving that job and more money. I now release my request to your loving hands and know that you will give me this or something better. Thank you."

When you don't surrender, you automatically limit your options because you are seeing the problem through *your* eyes and not God's. What I have experienced is that God always has a better idea for me. Many times those ideas have come through my wife or other people. Although I may feel out of control, when I surrender I ultimately have a sense of safety. So, ask for what it is you want out of life, relationships and God. And then surrender the means to God.

When I first moved to Houston from Seattle, I had a hard time creating money. I needed to start my spiritual counseling practice, but I was also full of fear at being rejected. And so, for a while, I stayed stuck. I remember praying and praying to God to "Please send me money. Please, please, God, send me more money." And then one day, I was reading the lesson in *A Course in Miracles* that states,

I do not perceive my own best interests.

Workbook Lesson 24

I suddenly realized that I was assuming that **I** knew what was best for me. I was assuming that money would solve my problems. That day I turned my prayers around and began to pray to God,

*"Dear God, help me to remove **my** barriers to more prosperity. Help me to open more to Your love."*

I began to take responsibility for the prosperity in my life. I was the one with barriers — not God. Three days later I got an answer. A friend that I owed $600 to called me from Seattle. As we were talking, he told me that he was inspired by my courage to move to a new city and start over. He was inspired by my example, and so, as a gesture of love, he was forgiving me the $600 debt.

After we hung up I saw the wonderful answer to my prayers. Though it didn't come in the form I expected (cash in the hand), it was a lessening of my debt load. And I saw that God was telling me that He was there to help, but I still had to go out there and create business. I still had to push through my fear. That day I stopped waiting for my fear to disappear and began to pursue my career with a new vigor.

Surrender relaxes the stress around trying to control your life. When I surrender to God, I feel like I have a partner with me. Somebody who will give me the right idea when it is needed. Somebody who is looking out for me.

One night, I remember driving to my Wednesday meeting feeling empty and scared. It seemed as if I was running out of ideas for speeches and that my creative well was drying up. I was having thoughts that I couldn't go on, that I needed to quit. I was rushing to my class, because I was late, when I got behind a car that just would not move out of my way — a big, slow, "stupid" car — and I couldn't pass. I began to get angry. And the angrier I got, the less the traffic cooperated. Suddenly a thought crossed my mind.

"There are no accidents. There is a reason for this car being in your way."

So I slowed down, took a breath and then I noticed the bumper sticker. It said,

"Don't quit! Surrender!"

I laughed and immediately relaxed. Instead of trying to get to class on time, fighting the traffic all the way, I decided to let God be in charge. If I was supposed to be late, well, I would just let whatever lesson I needed to learn come up. Of course, once I relaxed and surrendered, the traffic opened up and I made it to class in plenty of time. I also had my topic to teach that night.

When I am using Breath Integration with a client, there actually comes a point where, if the client can surrender, the body actually relaxes and the feeling that seemed so enormous a minute ago is now accepted. This is called a *breath release*. The person may still be in fear or low self esteem, but there is an acceptance and actually a joy as the person realizes that the feeling means nothing about them. I have seen clients, locked up in fear, who continue to breathe through a session, and suddenly hit this point. It's not dramatic, so it can easily slip by you, but if you're alert, you realize that the fear no longer seems to fill the room. The person is actually coming to peace with the feeling in question.

When we surrender, we allow new ideas and lessons into our lives. One of my biggest lessons in surrendering was around my wife. When we first got into a relationship, Stav had told me that she loved receiving roses and that she always wanted to receive a diamond solitaire ring from a man. I remember my initial thought,

"The roses I can see, but the diamond ring — there's **no way** she'll ever get that!"

You see, there was this angry little boy inside that was not going to give her what she wanted — no matter what! I had this thought that once you give a woman a diamond, then she wants a fur coat, and then a Mercedes, and then a new house, and then a trip to Hawaii, and then... and then... and on and on. I had these really *good* reasons for not giving her what she wanted. Or so I thought.

Then one year, on one of her birthdays, I decided to throw a surprise party. I asked each of the guests to bring at least one rose as a gift. I had never thrown a surprise party for anyone and I was all excited with the thought of the house being filled with people and roses. And then I had this absolutely horrible thought,

"What if," it whispered, "you bought her a diamond ring for her birthday?"

"No way!" I replied. "Besides, we don't have enough money, so it's useless even thinking about it."

"But *what if* there was a ring you could afford?" (The Holy Spirit can be very persuasive at times.)

And so I surrendered to the thought of buying her a ring. I let myself feel what it would mean to buy this gift. What came up in me was all of the suppressed emotions I had around past relationships. I began to feel angry at women in my past, whom I had bought lots of gifts and then the relationship didn't last. I felt angry for all the times I gave my love and it wasn't received. A part of me was screaming,

"No! I'll never be that open again. I always get hurt!"

I began to realize the real reason I had resistance to giving her what she wanted — I was still hurting and angry from past relationships. But Stav was the one paying for those past relationships.

So, with all those feelings churning inside, I decided to go to Macys, to see if possibly there was something I could buy. As it turned out, I just *happened* to go on the day they were having their annual diamond sale. And, of course, I found a small solitaire ring that I could afford and I went ahead and bought it.

The day before the party my fears arose.

"What if she doesn't like it? What if it's too small? What if she just laughs in my face?"

And then my ego kicked in.

"Wimp! You sold out, boy. She's really got you wrapped around her little finger! A real **man** wouldn't have given her anything!"

Luckily I called my friend Phil Smedstad, who always sees the divine in any situation, and within two minutes he had me laughing.

"Let's see, Jerry. You're throwing a surprise party for your wife, which you've never done before. You're going to buy her two dozen roses and everybody else is bringing roses. And you bought her a diamond ring. You've never done that before either. Do you think that *maybe* you're just a *little* activated, being so far out of your comfort zone?"

I took a breath and laughed,

"Well. . . maybe."

"You're doing fine, Jerry. You're just scared and your ego's going nuts. You're safe."

The party, the next day, was wonderful. Stav walked into a house filled with people and roses. She was thrilled to see all those people, she was thrilled with the gifts and she loved the ring.

We both agreed, later, that it was the happiest day of our lives together since our wedding day. It actually felt wonderful to give to my wife at that level. And through this experience I felt a lessening of the past pain. I felt a love for my old relationships and I realized that they too received every gift of love I gave. I realized that they had loved me too. The relationships just didn't work out.

That's all. It didn't mean anything about me, my gifts or our love. It just didn't work the way we expected.

What have I learned around surrendering? I have learned that women are safe, that God is safe **and** that I am safe. I have learned to open up more to myself and others. I have felt a lessening of my old defenses and a more openness to love. The feelings and release I felt in buying that ring were worth much more than the cost.

It's a pretty ring. It may not be the Hope diamond, but it has given me more hope for myself and relationships. And you know what? She'll get more roses — and diamonds.

Affirmations

- *It is safe to surrender to my relationship because it is safe to surrender to me.*

- *When I surrender to my relationship, I surrender to God.*

- *God is always giving me more than I ask. I cannot lose.*

- *God only wants the best for me.*

- *I am open, flexible and teachable.*

- *Learning to surrender is easy.*

- *My relationship only wants the best for me.*

- *My boss only wants the best for me.*

- *I only want the best for me.*

- *I now let God do some of the work in my life.*

- *God is always talking to me and I am always willing to listen.*

*Instead of everything falling apart,
maybe it's all falling together.*

Rev. Lura Smedstad

*One day as several of us students were with
our teacher visiting a state park. As we
stood at a point overlooking the beautiful
view, our teacher pointed to a pile of
garbage below us.*
"Your perception is a lot like this place.
*You can see the garbage and notice the
view.*
*Or you can notice the garbage and see the
view."*

Rev. Debrorah Olsen

*Because I am not moved by appearances,
appearance move.*

Catherine Ponder

*Thank God not every prayer is answered,
or I would have married the wrong man
several times.*

Ruth Graham (Billy Graham's wife)

Light, Smoke and Mirrors

Have you ever gone to a magic show? Ever wonder how all those wonderful tricks are done? Well, it's all done with light, smoke and mirrors which are used to distract us away from what the magician does not want us to see. They are used to portray something that isn't there. They are used to fool us.

I remember once in a business meeting when somebody asked the presenter how he got through a particular touchy subject and he responded that he did it with the help of a lot of light, smoke and mirrors. In other words, he BS'd the audience.

The ego is always invested in getting us to believe in the appearances of the world because it knows that as long as we are busy fighting what's "out there" we will never look at what is really going on inside. You see, when you begin to invest your belief in your true Self, you will begin to see that the world is illusory, that appearances aren't always as they appear. That there are a lot of light, smoke and mirrors.

When Buddha became enlightened, he said that the world is "maya" or illusion. What he meant by this is not so much that the world we see is a dream (which it is) but that "Since the world does not affect me, it might as well be a dream." What he was saying was that,

"Yes, you can hurt or kill my body, but you cannot affect who I believe I am, unless I choose to let you."

Now this doesn't mean that since the world is an illusion, that we should just ignore or deny it. You see, for whatever reason, we have decided to be here – in this dream. It doesn't make us or the dream bad. As *A Course in Miracles* says, the purpose of the *Course* is to help you to change your nightmare into a happy dream and gradually trust that it is safe to wake up. So go ahead, have relationships, buy cars, make money, enjoy life but just remember as Jesus once told us,

"Be in the world, not of it."

Enjoy the dream but always remember that there is another way of seeing everything.

So if the world is an illusion, how is it that situations in our life *seem* so real? It is because we invest our belief and energy into it. For example, it has been shown that the average millionaire has gone bankrupt six to eight times. Six to eight times these people lost all of their money and yet they tried again and again until ultimately they reached their goal. Now if I went bankrupt, the experience might be devastating to me. But to these people it didn't stop them. Why? Because they did not give the experience any power over their reality. They did not let the experience of bankruptcy affect whether they would reinvest or try again. They had the belief that "It's only money," and they picked themselves up and took whatever steps necessary to get back on their feet.

There comes a point in everybody's evolution in which we are tempted by the illusions in the world. We lose a job and we are tempted to believe that losing that job actually means anything about us. A relationship ends and we are tempted to believe that the end of the relationship means that we are losers. Now granted, there are lessons to be learned from the experience. Where did we go wrong? What errors did I make? What do I need to change? But regardless of the lessons, it is our belief that will determine whether we will make this experience real to us or just another experience.

When we begin to believe that we are losers because a relationship ends, we are actually investing a part of our spirit and energy into financing that belief. This gives the belief *energy and life*. We are now beginning to make the belief more real. And as you give that belief more energy, you will begin to act as if that belief is true. And so now you begin to act like a loser. Your shoulders slump, you don't make eye contact with people, you slouch through life, expecting nothing and getting to be right.

Earlier I related how I worked at Krogers, bagging groceries, after trying for months to get a computer programming job. Well, after a few weeks bagging groceries, I finally had an interview and then one morning, Peter, the man who was interviewing me for a position, called me to set up a second interview. He wanted to know if I could meet him and his partner at 4:00 that afternoon.

"Boy," I said, "that'll be hard. My wife has the car and I'm working this afternoon at Krogers. Would tomorrow work?"

"Not really," Peter replied. "I really want my partner to talk to you, and he's going out of town tomorrow for the holidays. Maybe we should just plan to meet next week."

Something in my body immediately told me to act now, no matter how things looked. I took a deep breath and said,

"OK, I'll be there at 4:00."

"But you don't have a car. How will you get here?"

"I don't know but I'll be there."

When I got off the phone I immediatcly called my supervisor at Krogers and related the situation. I had earlier told her that I was in the process of interviewing for other jobs and that at times I would have to leave earlier. She was fine with me leaving earlier and got a replacement. Then I called a friend, to see if I could borrow her car. She said yes, she'd be glad to help.

And so at 2:00, she drove over to the store and picked me up. As I drove her back to her home she related how I was in luck, that the car had broken down last week and it had just been fixed.

I shot home, showered, dressed in my best suit and then sped out the door. It was a hot, spring day and so I had the air conditioner going full blast. As I was going through downtown Houston though, I began to notice that the car was acting funny. The radio began going in and out and the air conditioning was getting sporadic. I looked at the dashboard for any warning signs or lights. Nothing, except that the gas gauge was dropping noticeably. Fearing maybe I was burning too much gas too fast, I turned off the radio and air conditioning and rolled down the windows. Now I'm worrying and hot.

I was about four miles from my interview and the gas gauge was on empty and so I chugged into a gas station to fill up. It only took $2 worth of gas.

"Uh-Oh!" I thought.

I tried to start the car. Nothing.

I went over to the owner of the gas station and asked if he could give my car a jump. We connected the cables and the car started fine but when I closed the hood, the car died. Somewhere I had a short circuit. We tried two more times, with the same result. By now I am soaked in sweat, my hands are filthy and I'm about ready to give up. But I am only four miles away! I can smell this job! I turned to the owner and asked him,

"Could I borrow your car for a few hours. I'm only going to Memorial City, right down the road."

"No!" he replied.

"I'll pay you!"

"How much?"

"Twenty dollars. But I don't have the money on me now and I'll have to pay with a check when my wife gets here. But I'll give you anything to hold as collateral."

He seemed uncertain. I pulled out my Sears charge card and license for identification.

"When will you be back?"

"In two, two and a half hours."

"OK." He gave me his keys as I gave him my charge card and grabbed my suit coat, got in the car and charged off to my interview.

I arrived about 30 minutes early and so I went into the bathroom to assess the damage. My hair has messed, my hands black, my tie was askew and my shirt was soaked in sweat. I looked in the mirror as I purposely washed my hands slowly and repeated to myself,

"This is not real. I do not believe this has *any affect* on my life or my ability to get this job."

As carefully and lovingly as I could (my heart was still going a mile a minute) I cleaned up, adjusted my clothes and went into Peter's office. I asked the receptionist whether I could borrow the phone to call my wife. I got in contact with her and related where she could meet me when she got off work.

The interview went great. Peter's partner liked me and the other programmer liked me. After talking to both of them I was ushered into Peter's office.

"You know," Peter started, "I've never known anybody who had no idea how they would get to a job and then commit like you did. Even if you couldn't make it today, I still would have had you back. I also like the fact that you don't think you're too good to bag groceries. And," he motioned to my hands, "It's obvious that you're not afraid to get your hands dirty. Frankly, I'm impressed."

"Well," I replied, "Do you want to be more impressed?"

"Yeah."

"The car I started out for this interview is not the car I arrived in."

"What!" he said, wide-eyed. "How did you get here?"

And I told him my adventure along the way.

Needless to say, I got the job. Also, when I went back to settle accounts with the gas station owner, I was making out the check to him and asked him his name. He spelled it for me and then suddenly said,

"Oh make it out for ten dollars!"

At any point I could have believed the light, smoke and mirrors of the appearances. It was one of the many experiences I have had that things are never as they seem.

What I have also learned is that our intentions, determination and desire are what fuel our lives. That success does not depend on the *right* conditions or a *lucky* choice. It is our intention that points the way and guides us. Our determination that keeps us on track, no matter what. And our desire that keeps the dream alive. These are the secrets of creating the life and relationships that you want.

Growing up spiritually requires that we see past the worlds tricks of lights, smoke and mirrors. You will never know what is possible until you let go believing what you *think* is going on, and instead remember that there is always another loving and compassionate way to look at your life. Walk through the smoke of fear and uncertainty, and look in the mirror of your true self. And when you do . . . you will see Light.

Affirmations

- *I no longer let the world determine what I can or cannot do.*

- *I lovingly and firmly withdraw my investment in negative thoughts and appearances. I no longer give them any power.*

- *I am the determiner of any situation that I find myself.*

- *Since God is infinite, there are infinite possible solutions to any problem.*

- *I no longer limit my problem solving solely to my own intellect. There is a Wisdom within and around me that I can easily access.*

- *My problems are never as bad as they seem.*

- *Nothing that happens in the world can affect who I really am. I always remember my true source and divinity.*

- *There is always another way of looking at my life.*

*With the fearful strain that is on me
night and day,
if I did not laugh I should die.*
Abraham Lincoln

*I have some good news and
I have some bad news.
The bad news is that there is no key
to the universe.
The good news is —
it's never been locked.*
Steve Baerman as *Swami Beyondananda*

He who laughs — lasts.
Norwegian Proverb

*The national pastime of Tahiti
is making love,
but we, silly fools,
picked baseball.*
Bob Hope

The God of Laughter

Many years ago I saw a poster of Jesus, His head thrown back, hands on His heart and laughing an uproarious laugh.

"How blasphemous!" I thought.

A few months later, though, I began to like the poster. I had never entertained the idea of Jesus having a sense of humor and once I got over my initial reaction, I actually liked the picture.

When we are on the path back to our hearts, back to God, humor plays an important part. Since we are in a world based on perceptions, we are constantly surprised, upset, and jolted out of our normal way of thinking.

A Course in Miracles says that the Son of God (us) created all this pain and trouble when he forgot to laugh at himself. At some point, we thought we separated from God. We thought that by rebelling against God, we had hurt Him and He was going to punish us. And ever since that day, we have been in fear and pain, waiting for retaliation. God has never been hurt and we cannot or will not hurt Him because we truly love Him. But we thought that our rebellion was real. And we forgot to laugh. We didn't just *notice* the thought and let it go. And from that painful thought of separation we created a world based on separation, where people live their lives in fear and think they have to always protect themselves from something *out there*.

According to *A Course in Miracles*, a miracle is a change in perception. Remember that it is our thoughts that create the world we see. As we change our minds, we change our world. When we change our perception of the world around us, miracles occur, because now new outcomes are now possible. Some examples of miracles are:

- Seeing your parents in a new way.
- Forgiving an old hurt.
- Healing an argument with a loved one.

- Seeing another person's side to an issue.
- Curing oneself of cancer.
- Creating that unexpected financial windfall.
- Feeding the hungry.
- Raising the dead.

It's a change in perception, nothing more. When we perceive our parents differently, it becomes easier to forgive. When we perceive women differently, it becomes easier to relate. When we perceive our bodies differently, we begin to love and accept them. When we perceive our past differently, we release guilt and can thereby cure our bodies. Remember that it is our minds that affect the world, not the other way around. When I changed my mind about my mother, when I began to perceive her as a person, instead of who I *thought* she was, my relationships with women improved. Now I have the kind of relationship I've always wanted. And that, in my opinion, took a miracle.

A Course in Miracles tells us that miracles are natural, that they should be occurring all the time and that we should always be in a state of "miracle readiness". What this means is that we should be ready to change our minds about **anything** in a moment's notice. When you change your mind, you change your perception and thereby change your world. That is also why *A Course in Miracles* stresses that there are no such thing as a "big" miracle and a "little" miracle. They are all equally effective because they all start in the mind.

In my opinion, telling jokes is a form of miracle working. Isn't it true that the reason something is funny is because of a sudden shift in perception? We see one view of a particular problem and then suddenly — WHAP!! we are presented with a totally unexpected view, one that is equally true and valid. Isn't it also true that humor can lighten any situation and help the people involved to see issues differently?

My father is wonderful in changing people's perceptions with laughter. Dad loves to watch TV wrestling. (Actually secretly sometimes I do too. I get a certain enjoyment from the bravado, the strutting and the bad acting). My brother-in-law, Ted, could never understand it.

One day Ted comes walking into my dad's house while my dad is watching wrestling.

"Joe! What're you watching that junk for? Don't you know it's all fake? It's all acting!"

And my dad looks up slowly, with this dawning look in his eyes and says,

"Oh! And movies like *Star Wars* are real!"

It stopped Ted in his tracks. He looked at dad and laughed.

"OK, Joe. I get the message."

The more we can laugh at ourselves, at our conditions, the less serious life becomes. Arguments dissolve, mistakes can be corrected and forgiveness is easier. I read a story about a man who was speeding in Alabama when he was pulled over by a state trooper. The trooper sidled up to the car, his ticket book open, and said,

"I've been waitin' all day for you, boy."

"Well, I got here as fast as I could," The driver responded.

He got off with just a warning.

God is a God of love, of joy and, I believe, of laughter. There is no situation that can stand up to a good belly laugh. During the Cold War with Russia, there was a tense meeting between the Americans and the Soviets. The Russian ambassador looked at the blank, stern faces and started the meeting with a question.

"Do you know the difference between communism and capitalism?"

Nobody was willing to reply.

"Well, in capitalism, man exploits man. In communism — it's the other way around."

The members burst into laughter and the tense atmosphere was lifted.

Laughter softens the blows of a sometimes hard life. It can give you the fortitude to try that project just one more time, to believe in yourself once more and to see the world with gentler eyes. I remember a time when I was processing my life very deeply. I was depressed, scared and angry, and it felt as it would never change. My teacher, Joe, told me,

"Jerry, a year from now, you'll laugh about all this."

You know what? A year later I *was* laughing about those very same incidents. The only thing that changed was that some time had passed and I was able to see those same conditions with a different perspective, a new perception. In other words, I created a miracle. And since it is my choice to decide how I want to feel at a given moment, I decided to see if I could speed up the time it took for me to laugh at a situation. And the time it took to reconcile a situation began to shorten.

So now, whenever my life looks bleak, I tell myself,

"If I'm going to laugh about this a year from now, why wait 365 days?"

Now when I am confronted with what looks like the end of the world, I ask myself,

"Can I laugh about this a month from now? A week from now? Tomorrow? An hour from now? Can I change my perception now?"

Be willing to laugh more in your life. Be willing to change your perceptions of the world. You'll be happier and so will the world.

Affirmations

- *The more I laugh at my life, the easier it becomes.*

- *It is easy for me to smile.*

- *I love seeing new sides of myself.*

- *The bigger the problem, the more I laugh.*

- *Life is as easy as I choose.*

- *I see only joy because I am joy.*

- *I am willing to take myself lightly.*

- *No problem is too big for God.*

- *No problem is too big to laugh at.*

- *Since I will laugh about my problems a year from now, I now give myself permission to laugh now.*

"I can forgive, but I cannot forget,"
is only another way of saying
"I cannot forgive."

Henry Ward Beecher, *Life Thoughts*

Beware of the man
who does not return your blow;
he neither forgives you
nor allows you to forgive yourself.

George Bernard Shaw

It's hard to walk forward
when you're constantly looking back.

Jerome Stefaniak

Unforgiveness is like giving somebody
free rent in your head.

Anonymous

He that cannot forgive others,
breaks the bridge
over which he must pass himself;
for every man has need
to be forgiven.

Lord Herbert

Creating a New Future

What is it that keeps us creating the same lesson over and over? It's when we drag our past with us, wherever we go, always expecting the same thing to happen in the future. And when we expect the same future, we begin to prepare for it, we begin to act *as if* that future will come to pass, and ultimately we get to be right — we get the same future. For example; let's say that your past relationships always ended bitterly. They started out wonderfully, but always ended in pain and sorrow. When you create a new relationship, what you may probably subconsciously be saying to yourself is,

"Yeah, she's great now. But once we really get to know each other, then the fur will fly."

And from that standpoint, your relationship is already beginning to die. Unless you change your mind about the future of your relationship, you will be preparing for that day when the "fur will begin to fly." You'll be expecting any day to break up. With an expectation so strong — who can lose? Only you.

How does one break out of this bind? How does one create a new future? The magic word is — forgiveness.

As long as we inhabit a world filled with your perceptions versus my perceptions, forgiveness will be needed. When you forgive a person for past deeds in a relationship, what that does is open up a new future. By not dragging those old experiences into your new relationship, you give yourself the opportunity to expect only the best in the relationship. It may take many times to forgive a particular person, but each time you forgive, it's a step closer to God. It's a step closer to you.

How can you forgive?

The first step is to determine whether you are ready to forgive or not. If you are not ready, admit it. There's no sin in that. That is as good a place to start as any. *A Course in Miracles* says that true forgiveness means that you can acknowledge that nothing wrong was ever done in the first place. Now this can seem like a tall order to fill, and I agree. That is why forgiveness takes time. So if you are not ready to forgive, then ask yourself if you are *willing* to forgive. Or even if you are *willing* to be *willing* to forgive. I feel that all too often people forgive too quickly. They forgive in their **heads**, but not in their **hearts**. Too many times I have heard statements like,

"I forgave my ex-husband years ago — the stupid jerk!"

If there is still any negative feeling attached to a person or incident, just know that forgiveness is not yet complete. This is an area that will ask all of your compassion for yourself, because forgiveness may take months, even years to complete.

So what I support you in doing is to just be *willing* to forgive that person. Give yourself time to feel. Once you tell yourself that *someday* you will forgive this person, your divinity jumps up and says "Yippee!", because it knows that forgiveness is now inevitable, whether it be two months, two years, two decades or twenty lifetimes. Your divinity knows that you will get to a place where you totally release the pain and hurt. But in the meantime, do something about the pain and hurt. Get counseling, join a support group, work on your anger. Until the old feelings have been addressed and honored, forgiveness will stay out of reach.

Yes, we do like to hold onto old hurts, because, well, it's fun to drag them out every now and then and show them to people. It's fun to try to enroll the world in how hard done by we are, or how horrible our ex-wives were. But staying in the rage, the judgments, and the righteousness, is too painful. It impacts every day of our lives and brings more misery. If you let yourself trust the process of forgiveness, you will begin to feel a lessening of the pain.

A Course in Miracles states beautifully what unforgiveness looks like. It says that when you are unwilling to forgive a certain person, you are holding that person in prison. You want your beliefs about that person to stay a certain way and you don't want them to change. And if other people see your prisoner differently, well, you will then try to convince them how dangerous and horrible that inmate is. For example, have you ever been to a party and somebody begins to talk about an ex-lover in glowing terms? Have you ever said, or been tempted to say,

"Well if you knew her like I do, you wouldn't think she was so great! She can't cook, she doesn't keep her word and she's a liar."

You want to keep that prisoner jailed and you want others to dislike her too. But there is a price to pay by acting like this.

A Course in Miracles continues by saying that a warden of a prison is just as much a prisoner, because the warden needs to always be on guard — to make sure that the prisoners never escape or are shown any kind of love. And so warden and prisoners are both imprisoned.

How do you know that you are forgiving a person? One indicator is that your life will begin to reflect more peace. Another is that you will begin to remember pleasant, forgotten incidents. I spent years being angry at my mother. Even though I *thought* that I had forgiven, my relationships with women were still rocky because I had only forgiven her in my head and not my heart. At that time, forgiveness was just a *good idea*. But then I gave myself permission to start over, to not forgive her but to be willing to forgive. I let myself feel my rage for as long as it served me, and slowly the pain and hurt began to lift.

I remember a milestone in my forgiveness process the day I was driving home from work and suddenly I had a memory of my mom teaching me how to waltz at a wedding. And instantly another memory returned around the sixteenth birthday party she had given me. I remembered the cake, the people and her gifts. I remembered my favorite foods she used to cook for me — fried chicken, pork chops, vegetables smothered with cheese. Tears ran down my face as I realized that I was feeling genuine love for her. I was beginning to appreciate the wonderful gift she was in my life.

These memories and perceptions of my mother were always in my mind, but my unforgiveness prevented me from seeing them. All I ever saw was *my side* to everything. But being willing to forgive softened my vision and allowed positive acts to be remembered. And so, along with my mother, I also learned to forgive myself.

Forgiveness is a process. Sometimes I find myself feeling angry over an incident I thought I forgave years ago. Just know that like peeling an onion, as we forgive, we uncover new layers. Sometimes different aspects of the same incident arise to be forgiven, so remember to love yourself at these times.

Forgiveness breaks up those old patterns that keep us stuck. When you forgive and release the past, the future becomes a blank slate. Anything can happen. Anything is possible. Give yourself a new future, give yourself a new chance — forgive.

Self Discovery Quiz

- *Are there any incidents that you have forgiven, but not forgotten?*

- *Do you still feel righteous or "done to" by others?*

- *What is the hardest thing you find to forgive in others? Do you in **any** way act that way yourself?*

- *What do you expect from life, based on your past experience? Would you like something different?*

- *Are you recreating negative, past experiences in your present life? If so, what needs to be forgiven in order to change the future?*

- *Right now, what is something you feel you would like to forgive yourself for?*

- *List five wonderful things your mother did for you.*

- *List five wonderful things your father did for you.*

- *List five wonderful things that you have done in your life.*

*God could not be everywhere
and therefore He made mothers.*

Jewish proverb

*Children begin by loving their parents.
As they grow,
they judge them.
Sometimes they forgive them.*

Anonymous

*Don't limit a child to your own learning,
for he was born in another time.*

Rabbinic saying

*We go to the beach.
I look at the sea.
My mother thinks I stare.
My father thinks I want to go in the water.
But I have my own little world.*

Amy Levy, 12-years-old

Creating Your Perfect Parents

When you were growing up, do you remember ever see-ing your mother or father doing something that you judged and saying to yourself, "I'll never be like that!"?

And so we begin our adulthood, trying to do everything differently than mom and dad did. But trying to do things the opposite of our parents perpetuates the same problem because we end up not being ourselves. Instead we become "not dad" or "not mom" but never "Jerry". We don't live our **own life** because we are too busy trying not to live our parent's lives. We are living life in *reaction* to our parents instead of living life in response to them.

There are things that our parents did that were absolutely perfect. And there were things our parents did that were not perfect, that were even wrong. Our job, as adults, is to sift out the good and keep it, and replace the bad with better examples. By not following their good examples, we lose the benefit of *their* experience and have to reinvent the wheel as we perform the same errors they performed. It is our own unforgiving attitude that prevents us from standing on our parents shoulders and extending even further into life. Forgiveness is realizing that they were perfect and imperfect — just like us.

So as we go through life, we need to create our perfect parents. Who is that? The perfect parent will be a mixture of many people, because nobody, short of Jesus or Buddha or any of the ascended Masters, has it all together. The perfect parent will be a model of the type of person we want to be, a mixture of the positive attributes we want in ourselves. My model for the perfect father is a mixture of many men. There is Gandhi for living his beliefs and principles, Jesus for His unconditional love and honesty, Sir Thomas More for his integrity, Martin Luther King for his courage, General George Patton for admitting his love of war, Clint Eastwood for his *"now you've pushed me over the line,"* and even the Terminator for his one track mind and determination to get the job done. These are all *aspects* that in some way I admire.

Creating the parental model that we want in our life is not about making our parents wrong. It's about claiming responsibility for our lives and doing whatever needs to be done to heal those hurt, lonely spots in our hearts. Our parents were as perfect as they could be. Unfortunately, they were not mind readers, they were not always caring, they had their own areas of growth, and they had their own pain. They, too, were the products of their upbringing. In short, they were human. Our job is not to turn our backs on them, but to acknowledge their gifts to us and release what didn't work in our relationships.

When I was growing up, my dad found it hard to compliment me. Sometimes he would say, "You did good that time," but never the words I secretly wanted to hear — "I'm proud of you. You're a success in my eyes." He was afraid that praising us would go to our heads and we would stop working for better grades, etc. You know what? It *would* have gone to our heads and it would have felt great!

But he loved us in his own way. Even though he got more loving and expressive through the years, it was never the *right* way. It was not how I wanted to be loved. Usually his love took the form of money. Every Christmas and birthday, I could be assured of receiving fifty dollars, and every Christmas and birthday I would judge my father's love.

"He only knows how to love with money."

Until one fateful Christmas when I received a card from my parents. I opened it up thinking,

"Here comes another fifty bucks."

The envelope contained only a card — no check.

"What!" I thought. "My dad doesn't love me anymore!"

Then it hit me. All those years I spent judging my dad's money, and yet, I always spent it. I always looked forward to it.

"So who's the one really not expressing his love? At least your dad shows it with money. What about you?"

I saw how much I was blocking my father's love by judging his gifts. Who was I to determine how my father wanted to love me? I realized that I liked his love, even in the form of money!

A few days later, a second card arrived from my parents. In it was a fifty dollar check.

"He does love me after all!" was my thought.

I called him that night and told him what had happened and we both had a good laugh over it. It seemed that this Christmas, he had been feeling extra loving towards all his children and he had sent all of us an extra card, just to say he loved us. The empty card just "happened" to arrive first.

So what does this have to do with creating your perfect parent? Well, there are things that we wished our parents would do, that they didn't know we needed or were not able to give. In creating your perfect parent, you become the parent you always wanted to have. Did you feel unacknowledged as a child? Begin acknowledging yourself, or ask a friend or lover to tell you five things they appreciate about you. Do you acknowledge your children, or are you unwittingly repeating your parents' patterns? Were you not held enough? Begin to hold yourself with love and compassion. Ask for and give hugs and affection. Find the people in your life that express the attributes you treasure and learn from them.

It's funny how life will always lead you home. Earlier I related how I felt my dad could never say the things I wanted to hear. I felt that my father had never acknowledged me as a man. And so, one spring, I decided to participate in a "Men's Initiation into Manhood" weekend workshop. It was a beautiful experience of having an elder man initiate us into the realm of manhood. Something I learned is that, according to American Indian tradition, a father cannot initiate a son into manhood because there is too intimate a tie. Only an elder, such as a grandfather, uncle or shaman can do it, and so, with the help of other loving men and an elder, I entered manhood.

A few weeks later, my father called to tell me that he had cancer and was going into the hospital for an operation. I phoned him the day after surgery and found out that the doctors had discovered the cancer early enough. All of the cancer had been removed without any after-affects. After the preliminary medical news and the normal chit-chat, I noticed that my father was having a hard time talking. He periodically had to stop, he said, to drink water because his throat was dry. But something told me that there was more going on and so I imagined my heart opening and loving him. He began to speak again and then suddenly he began to cry.

"You know, Jerry, when you were growing up, there were things I never told you because I was always afraid you would get too proud. But I want to tell you now. I've always been proud of you. It didn't matter that you got divorced, or lost your money or didn't have a job. I was still proud of you. You've always been a success in my eyes. I never stopped loving you. I'm glad you are my son. I love you."

We cried together, separated by 4,000 miles but joined at the heart.

A week later, at a men's group meeting, I was relating the story about my father, when one of the men replied,

"Of course that happened. You took responsibility to get yourself initiated into manhood and then your father initiated you himself."

Our parents are no longer responsible for how we feel about them, the world, or our relationships. It is up to us to decide what it is we want in life and to create it. It is our decision whether we want to continue creating the same relationships over and over, or whether we take the helm of life and steer our ship into new harbors.

Be yourself. Be happy. Be your own best parent.

Affirmations

- *I no longer wait for my parents to love me the way I want to be loved. I am the creator of the love in my life.*

- *I am now open to the gifts my parents gave me as a child.*

- *I now see my father and mother with new eyes.*

- *I now release what doesn't work in my relationships and I embrace what does.*

- *I now am willing to express my love to my relationship and my children.*

- *I love looking inside myself because there is only love inside.*

- *I now forgive my parents for all imperfect acts.*

- *I now forgive myself for all imperfect acts.*

- *As I forgive, so am I forgiven.*

- *I am now willing to remember the wonderful things I learned from my parents.*

*The best way to make
your dreams come true
is to wake up.*

Paul Valery

*After we have sought over the wide world,
you learn that happiness is to be found
only in your own home.*

Voltaire

*If you don't have a dream,
then how can your dream come true?*

Dr. Richard Diamond

*The greatest and noblest pleasure which
men can have in this world is to discover
new truths; and the next is to
shake off old prejudices.*

Fredrick the Great

Maybe This is Heaven

When people ask me, "Do you believe there is a Hell?" I always reply, "Yes I do! I've been there!" Hell is not a place. It's a state of mind. It is how we view the world and the people within.

It's my opinion that God could not create a hell worse than the hell we create in our own minds. Only I know myself intimately enough that I can torture myself in my own special way. Only I know those secret avenues of self doubt. And I can rack myself with guilt, anger and shame better than any person I know, and do it 24 hours a day, seven days a week. No relationship ever made me feel worse than how I treated myself. I have created people who helped bring up those hellish feelings of hate, shame and anger, but nobody can bring up a hell in another, *unless it is already there.*

When I began my journey back to God, back to love, I had a lot of fear of looking at what I *thought* was lurking in my heart. As I uncovered layer after layer of unlovable thoughts, I became more convinced that I really was bad, a monster, that I was a sinner. I was certain that there a an "Alien" lurking in my heart, waiting to leap out and hurt others. Luckily, though, I had friends and teachers who never stopped seeing the truth about me. They supported me to press on, to continue looking within, even in the depths of despair.

One day I opened *A Course in Miracles Workbook* to the lesson for that day. The lesson was,

There is no cruelty in God, and none in me.

Workbook Lesson 170

I read it and began to cry. I was so convinced that I was cruel and mean, and here was a lesson that affirmed that not only was God not cruel, but neither was I. I felt a sadness all day, a sadness in surrendering to the thought that I was greater than I ever realized. I had to look at every little way I judged myself, every "sin" I ever committed and in the face of that evidence, I still acknowledged that there was no cruelty in God and none in me. It was a day I began to feel reborn. Jesus said that the kingdom of Heaven is within — and so also resides the kingdom of hell.

A few years ago I was at Disneyland with my wife. As we waited at the gates, we were surrounded by a mob of smiles — each person was excited and happy to be there. But as the gates opened and we walked in, I noticed a teenager with this angry scowl on his face. Maybe he was having a bad day. Maybe his father yelled at him earlier. Maybe he just hated Disneyland. But the thing is that here was an opportunity to let go and still enjoy life, but he was deciding to hang onto the negative feelings a little longer. I thought,

"Isn't that just like people? . . . Isn't that just like me!"

How many times have I let an argument or a misperception to get in my way? How many weekends have I spoiled because I got angry at a lover and would not let it go? How many experiences have I cheated myself out of because I would not budge from my way of looking at something? And was it worth hanging onto those feelings at the expense of a deeper and fuller life? I think not.

We forget that this world is a playground where we can learn and play. And in this playground there are people who work and play, people who sell hot dogs, sweep up and still make time to ride the rides; and people who sell hot dogs, sweep up and grumble about how hard life is. They never even give themselves the time to ride the rides. We can be in heaven and never acknowledge it.

The movie *Field of Dreams* is about forgiveness and the possibility of seeing Heaven on earth. After Ray listens to the Voice, trusts, builds the baseball field and meets Shoeless Joe, there is a scene where Shoeless Joe is leaving to disappear into the cornfield. Halfway across the field, he turns around and yells,

"Hey! Is this Heaven?"

And Ray replies, confused, "No. It's Iowa."

Then at the end of the movie, Ray meets his dad and his dad asks the same question.

"Is this Heaven?"

"No," replies Ray, quizzically. "It's Iowa."

"I could have sworn it was Heaven," mumbles his dad.

Ray thinks a moment and then asks,

"Is there a Heaven?"

"Oh yes. It's the place where dreams come true."

And Ray looks around, at the beautiful sunset, the farm, the house, his wife and daughter playing and laughing on the porch. And he smiles.

"Maybe *this* is Heaven," says Ray.

Give yourself the opportunity to repeat throughout your day, "Maybe this is Heaven," and see if your world begins to change for the better.

If you find little aspects of hell, here and there, remember to see yourself with compassion and acknowledge, "This is just another part of myself coming up to be healed. I am still in Heaven because I *am* Heaven." And then do whatever you need to do to process that piece of hell, but love yourself along the way. And remember that you have help. Jesus says in *A Course in Miracles*,

*When I said "I am with you always," I meant it literally. I am not absent to anyone in any situation. Because I am always with you, **you** are the way, the truth and the life.*

Text 107/116

The state of the world will always reflect the state of your mind. Let yourself be wrong about everything you thought you knew about life. Let yourself believe that you are a child of God and soon you will find yourself at home, in heaven.

Affirmations

- *Heaven is a state of mind and I am in a heavenly state.*

- *I am now vigilant only for God's kingdom.*

- *Love is all around and I now see it.*

- *I am worthy of creating my dreams.*

- *I deserve all the love God has in store for me.*

- *The more I see Heaven, the more Heaven sees me.*

- *I am a heavenly being.*

- *I now embrace my divinity with peace, joy and acceptance.*

- *I now receive the gifts God wants to give me through others.*

- *I now see Heaven in others.*

The day will come when, after harnessing the winds, the tides, and gravitation, we shall harness for God the energies of love. And on that day, for the second time in the history of the world, man will have discovered fire.

Teilhard de Chardin

One day a classmate asked him what had caused him to become so badly crippled. "Infantile paralysis," said the young man on crutches.
"With a misfortune like that," said the friend, "how can you face the world so confidently and happily?"
"Because," replied the polio victim, "the disease never reached my heart."

Edward Gibbon

May the "Course" be with you.

Jerry Stefaniak

More Compassionate Truths About You

(From *A Course in Miracles*)

- *You are the work of God, and His work is wholly lovable and wholly loving. This is how a man must think of himself in his heart, because that is what he is.*

    Text 7/9

- *Rebirth is merely the dawning on your mind of what is already in it.*

    Text 86/94

- *Your worth is not established by teaching or learning. Your worth is established by God. Nothing you do or think or wish or make is necessary to establish your worth.*

    Text 49/55

- *Deep within you is everything that is perfect, ready to radiate through you and out into the world.*

    Workbook 63/63

- *You are altogether irreplaceable in the Mind of God. No one else can fill your part of it, and while you leave your part empty your eternal place merely waits for your return.*

    Text 167/180

- *To accept your littleness is arrogant, because it means that you believe your evaluation of yourself is truer than God's.*

  Text 167/180

- *There is a place in you where there is perfect peace. There is a place in you where nothing is impossible. There is a place in you where the strength of God abides.*

  Workbook 76/76

- *. . . understand what "the Kingdom of Heaven is within you" really means . . . the word 'within' is unnecessary. The Kingdom of Heaven is you.*

  Text 54/60

- *Your passage through time and space is not at random. You cannot but be in the right place at the right time.*

  Workbook 65/65

- *God does not change His mind about you, for He is not uncertain of Himself . . . When anything threatens your peace of mind, ask yourself, "Has God changed His mind about me?"*

  Text 163/175

- *Say to yourself "God Himself is incomplete without me."*

  Text 165/178

- *Child of God, you were created to create the good, the beautiful, and the holy. Do not forget this.*

  Text 12/15

*There's this little wave, this he-wave,
who's bobbing up and down, off the shore,
bobbing up and down on the ocean, having
a great time, and all of a sudden he
recognizes he's going to crash into the shore
. . . and he'll get annihilated. And he gets
so depressed.*

*"My God," he thinks, "what's going to
happen to me?"*

*And he's got this sour, despairing look
on his face.*

*Along comes a she-wave, bobbing up
and down, having a great time. And the
she-wave says to the he-wave,*

"Why are you so depressed?"

*"You don't understand!" says the he-
wave. "We're going to crash into the shore!
We'll be nothing!"*

*"Silly Boy!" replies the she-wave.
"Don't you understand? You're not a wave.
You're the ocean."*

Morrie Schwartz

*Action may not always bring happiness;
but there is no happiness without action.*

Benjamin Disraeli

*Call on God, but row
away from the rocks.*

Indian Proverb

How to Use Affirmations

Affirmations have been an important tool in changing my life. Since we create with our minds, it is important to retrain our minds out of old, negative, self-sabotaging beliefs to beliefs that support a loving, abundant lifestyle. I have seen my life change dramatically from lack and struggle with relationships, to increased prosperity, loving, harmonious relationships and a greater sense of peace in my world. As the saying goes, "The mind is a terrible thing to waste." Let's use this powerful tool, not miscreate with it.

Some of the techniques I use are:

- Use your name when writing affirmations. This gets the attention of the mind easier. If you are doing work around your childhood or with your inner child, use the name you were called as a child. If you had a nickname, use that also.

- Repeat the affirmation throughout the day to constantly remind yourself of the new thought you want to embrace. Tell yourself on the way to work your new thought. Instead of cursing the traffic, repeat the affirmations. Saying them out loud also utilizes your ears. I also find that saying them in different voices (loud, soft, whisper, silly) enhances the introduction of the new idea.

- Writing the affirmation multiplies the benefit because it uses more of the body's senses. Remember, the more of the bodies senses that can be marshaled in your change, the quicker the message sinks in. Write the affirmation in the three tenses, or persons, five to ten times per day. For example,

I, Jerry, now accept myself.	(5 - 10 times)
You, Jerry, now accept yourself.	(5 - 10 times)
Jerry now accepts himself.	(5 - 10 times)

- Write the affirmations for at least a week.

- To see how your mind responds to these new ideas, you can write a response for each line you write. To do this, draw a line vertically on the page about one-third of the way from the right edge. This will be your "response column." When you finish writing a line of affirmation, write the **first** thought that pops into your mind. For example,

I, Jerry, now accept myself.	*What a lie!*
I, Jerry, now accept myself.	*I hate this!*
I, Jerry, now accept myself.	*I'm willing.*

When writing your response, don't edit your thoughts. Just write them as they are. Over time you can see how your resistance to the new idea is changing. When you get to a place where you notice no particular thought around an affirmation, neither good or bad, know that the thought has now been accepted into your thought system.

- Create a cassette tape with your affirmations on it. It is interesting and wonderful to hear your own voice telling you new thoughts about yourself, affirming the truth about who you are. You can then play it on the way to work, before sleeping or any other time. Use a five or ten minute "endless loop" cassette tape available at stores like Radio Shack.

- Don't be afraid to create your own affirmations. Look at the areas in your life that need change and start affirming what it is you desire in each situation. Do you want more peaceful relationships? Affirm that. Do you want increased prosperity? Affirm that. Look at the thoughts that are causing problems in your life and turn them around into positive, life affirming statements. If you think that there is never enough money, create an affirmation like, *"I now know that there is more than enough time, love and money for me."* If you have trouble coming up with ideas, ask your lover, your friends, your minister for help.

- Also begin to look around in your life where you may be creating **negative** affirmations. What do you think bumper stickers such as "Shit Happens!" affirm? I have a friend who was always complaining about her lack of money. One day I noticed something that she had printed on her checks - *"Money talks. Mine says* **good-bye***."* When I pointed this out, she quickly ordered a new set of checks and tossed the old ones out. On our checks, Stav and I have printed, *"God is the source of our abundance."* This helps to remind us and anyone who sees our checks that it is God, not our job or clients, who is the source of all our good.

As the affirmations begin to work, one of two things will happen;

· The situation will improve
   or
· The situation will appear to get worse

In either case, *do not* stop the affirmations. When things get better, we tend to think the work is done and then we stop, never realizing that the affirmation still needs a little more work to get inside. Continuing with the affirmation for another week cements the foundation you worked so hard to establish.

When things appear to get worse, remember that this, too, is *temporary*. As you work on expanding the Divine truth within you, it will push to the surface every unloving, lacking thought. As you become aware of these old thoughts, you can now release them, but first you must become aware of them. This is the time to persevere. Continue the affirmations **no matter what,** until you see a change. You *will* see a change because life is your tool, not your master.

Since affirmations bring to our consciousness any suppressed thoughts, they also bring up the feelings that are associated with those thoughts. Old thoughts that we are stupid, worthless and sleazy have charged emotions attached to them. It is not uncommon to feel sad, depressed or angry during this time. This too, is temporary. The feelings will pass as you reaffirm these new beliefs and begin experiencing a change in your outer world.

Learning about yourself is not a solitary process so, if possible, develop a support system. People who understand what you are going through can help immensely. Counselors, ministers, friends and support groups have been invaluable in my growth process. Many times I needed to hear a word of encouragement from somebody who experienced similar things or at least from someone who didn't believe in my littleness. As you grow, others will grow with you, and you can grow from their experience.

And remember, *you cannot do it wrong*. When you have the intention to heal yourself - you will! So use the affirmations in this book, or other books, or make up your own. God loves you and where there is a desire to go home, He will help.

Suggested Readings

These are just a few of the books that helped influence my life.

A Course in Miracles

Three books — a Text, a Workbook for Students and a Manual for Teachers — that explain who we really are, our purpose in the world and our part in God.

Intimacy in Action – Relationships That Feed the Soul by Jerome Stefaniak

A wonderful book that deals exclusively with relationships and written by my favorite author – me. It encompasses everything that Stav and I use in keeping our relationship alive, passionate, and exciting. This book will give you a better understanding of what relationships are for, why we get into the kinds of relationships we have, and how to get along with that special person you have decided to be with.

A Return to Love by Marianne Williamson

A wonderful explanation of the principles of *A Course In Miracles* in everyday terms and how to use them.

Forgiveness and Jesus by Kenneth Wapnick

Further explanation of *A Course in Miracles* and how forgiveness is the keystone to opening our lives to our magnificence.

Feel the Fear and Do It Anyway by Susan Jeffers

A primer, as far as I'm concerned, for anyone who wants to experience life fully. She has many exercises on how to see and deal with our fears. Excellent!

From a Chicken to an Eagle by Jerry Fankhauser

A small, easy to understand book about learning to claim who we really are.

Zen and the Art of Motorcycle Maintenance by Robert Pirsig

This book was required reading in one of my college courses and was one of the most important things I learned in college. A story of a man and his son not only on a cross country journey but on a journey into the heart. A book about finding the excellence in our lives and becoming one with our separated selves.

Chop Wood, Carry Water by Rick Fields, Peggy Taylor,
Rex Wyler & Rick Ingrasci

A mixed bag of different aspects of spirituality by the editors of *New Age Journal*. Very good if you are new to spiritual ideas. Enjoyable and easy reading.

Love Is Letting Go of Fear by Gerald Jampolsky

Principles of *A Course in Miracles* explained in a easy-to-understand format. He also relates in detail how our thoughts create the problems we see in the world and the diseases that we create in our own bodies.

Compassion and Self Hate by Theodore Isaac Rueben

The book that started it all for me! It details the many ways we suppress our aliveness by hating and criticizing ourselves. Not to leave us hanging, he also details how to begin to love and accept ourselves as people.

Everyday Zen by Charlotte Joko Beck

A wonderful book of short essays and talks about Zen. Packed with wonderful examples of embracing our spirituality and our humanity. This book is great reading for anyone interested in expanding their divinity, not just for people who do Zen meditation.

Unlocking the Power Within by Eric Butterworth

A book explaining the power that is within every one of us and how to open to it. A good book in explaining many metaphysical concepts.

The Anger Book by Theodore Isaac Rueben
> Another milestone in my reading career. This book chronicles how suppressed anger destroys our bodies, our relationships and our lives. If you think expressing your anger is bad, read this book and see how NOT expressing it affects your life.

The Nine Faces of Christ by Eugene E. Whitworth
> A fictional(?) account of the life and training of Christ through Jesus's eyes. A lot of explanation of the different religions at the times and what Jesus possibly experienced as He embraced His Divinity.

The Road Less Traveled by M. Scott Peck
> The road less traveled is the road into ourselves, the road we most fear. This book chronicles the benefits and joy we experience as we face the fear of who we *think* we are and realize who we *really* are.

Siddartha by Hermann Hesse
> The first time I read this book I merely enjoyed the story. The second time I read it slowly, like sipping a fine wine. It is the beautiful story of a young priestly man who realizes that enlightenment cannot be taught but only experienced. And so he proceeds to lose himself into life, to fully experience emotions, greed, materiality, sex and finally a fuller experience of love. I found myself having a deep sense of connection and love for life and God after reading this book.

The Lazy Man's Guide to Enlightenment by Thaddeus Golas
> Don't let the thinness of this book fool you! I found it jam-packed with wonderful deep material. I would read it, a paragraph at a time and let myself sense just what the author was saying. Wonderful!

The Most Fun You'll Ever Have Learning About Getting Along With People!

- *Have you ever had, what you thought was a perfect love relationship and then watched helplessly as it deteriorated into something else?*

- *Do you find yourself falling in love with the same kind of person, over and over, no matter how hard you try to get somebody different?*

- *Do you frequently get into the same kind of arguments that lead nowhere and accomplish nothing?*

- *Would you like to understand just why relationships are the way they are and why they drive us crazy?*

In *Intimacy in Action: Relationships That Feed the Soul*, Rev. Jerome Stefaniak gently and compassionately guides readers into the fertile, powerful, and sometimes frightening realm of healing possibilities that only relationships can provide. And he manages to build a bridge from the often lofty, detached world of spiritual principles to the rutty, bumpy, frustrating, challenging, exciting reality of day-to-day dealings among people. This is clearly much more than just another "communication skills" primer for couples.

Rev. Stefaniak's abundant use of personal examples is both instructive and inspiring. He provides specific examples and methods for breaking the repetitive and frustrating cycles of blame, distrust, and self-protection to reach win-win solutions

Relationships that are easy, loving, passionate, open and fun? What if this is truly possible for you? *What if?* Whether this question intrigues, excites, or annoys you, Rev. Stefaniak is the perfect person to lead you into a discovery of your unlimited possibilities to love.

You'll only wish you had discovered Rev. Stefaniak years ago!

As a member of a psychotherapist couple myself, and working with lots of couples, I see Jerry's book as a great, easy-to-read relationship companion, and one I will recommend to my clients.

Jerry Goodman, LMSW-ACP

I strongly recommend this book to people who want to follow the path of healing and growth that is available in relationships. I will certainly recommend this book to my client couples.

Gerald R. Oncken, Ph.D.,Counselor

In Intimacy in Action – Relationships that Feed the Soul, *Jerry Stefaniak offers the reader a new experience of forgiveness of him/herself and others. Inspired by* A Course in Miracles, *he masterfully blends spiritual principles into the everyday challenges of relationships. His own love of God and his appreciation of our humanness permeates his writing. This is a book that will help open your heart, and thus, receive the relationships of your dreams.*

Coky Gray

This is a very strong book. The author provides information and devices for introspection and self-discovery that really stand on their own. The author is an experienced relationship advisor and workshop leader and his information is valuable, authoritative, and well written. Rev. Stefaniak has created a well-written, easy-to-read, engaging book.

Book reviewer for Llewellyn Publishers

Title: *Intimacy in Action – Relationships that Feed the Soul*
Author: Jerome Stefaniak
ISBN: 1-887918-39-6
Retail Price: $16.95   **# Pages**: 288

A Course in Miracles
Overview

If you are interested in learning more about *A Course in Miracles*, there is no better way of understanding the concepts than by attending Jerry Stefaniak's classes. The next best thing is listening to his tapes. His six tape overview series on *A Course in Miracles* is an excellent resource for new and seasoned students of the *Course*. It covers the basic concepts of the *Course*, how it applies to your life, and practical support in using these ideas in your daily life. This series also includes his wonderful meditations.

Reverend Stefaniak uses humor, real down-to-earth, day-to-day examples and his own life to help the listener understand these wonderful and powerful lessons. Altogether, the tapes total about **nine hours** of spiritual and practical support. The topics covered are:

- *What Are Miracles?*
- *What Is the Ego?*
- *Love and Fear*
- *Releasing Judgements*
- *Creating Healthy Relationships*
- *Forgiveness*

If you would like to have Jerry speak at your organization about personal transformation or would simply like to comment on *Compassionate Living - Everyday Spirituality*, please forward your correspondence to:

Reverend Jerome Stefaniak
Inner Awakenings
11306 Overbrook, Houston TX 77077
(713) 785-3131

T o order *Intimacy in Action – Relationships that Feed the Soul,* the *Course in Miracles Tape Series,* or more copies of *Compassionate Living - Everyday Spirituality,* copy and send in the form below.

Please make checks payable to: Reverend Jerome Stefaniak

Ship to: _____

Name: _____

Address: _____

City, State, Zip: _____

Phone: _____ Fax: _____

Please write any special instructions on back.
Shipping is $4.
If ordering three or more items, there is no shipping charge.

_____ copies of *Intimacy in Action* at $16.95 each = _____

_____ copies of *Compassionate Living* at $14.95 each = _____

_____ sets of *Course* tapes at $45 each = _____

Total = _____

Shipping (if applicable) = _____

Grand Total = _____

Texas residents please add 8¼% Texas sales tax